CALLOUSED HANDS, COURAGEOUS SOULS

CALLOUSED HANDS, COURAGEOUS SOULS

Holistic Spirituality of Development and Mission

Robert J. Suderman

Translated by

W. Derek Suderman

MARC

A division of World Vision
800 West Chestnut Avenue, Monrovia, California 91016-3198
USA

ISBN 1-887983-11-2

MARC books are published by World Vision, 800 West Chestnut Avenue, Monrovia, California 91016-3198 U.S.A.

Printed in the United States of America. Editor and typesetter: Joan Weber Laflamme. Cover design: Steven J. Singley. Cover photo: D. C. Ritchie.

This book was originally published in Spanish as *Tengan Valor: Yo he Vencido al mundo; Espiritualidad y Misión,* © 1998 CLARA-SEMILLA and Vision Mundial.

To my wife, Irene,
companion on the road,
teacher of spirituality,
architect of mission,
engineer of justice—thank you.

Contents

Preface to the English Edition

This book was initially written in Spanish for a Latin American audience, and evidence of this fact will be found throughout the book. Only after its publication in Spanish was it suggested that its content might also be relevant for a North American audience. Some changes have been made. But most of the illustrations still come out of the Latin American experience and speak to it. When I felt apologetic about this, my friends reminded me that Latin Americans have for many years read materials written primarily for North American and European audiences, and these friends suggested that inverting this process may not be bad. This argument convinced me to allow publication of the book in English.

I hope this book can serve as a bridge, bringing the world of Latin America closer to North Americans. I pray for God's gracious guidance to understand what the text is attempting to say, and God's direction in knowing how to respond once we have understood.

—ROBERT J. SUDERMAN

Preface

I am pleased to offer this work, with the hope that reflection upon our context of suffering, our meditation on the Word of God, and the adrenaline, energy and encouragement this involves, will refresh us and give us much joy in our Christian walk.

I eagerly accepted the assignment to write a book about Christian spirituality and mission. However, upon applying myself to this subject, I soon felt small and insignificant, especially when I studied the great theologians and thinkers who have written so brilliantly throughout Christian history. Libraries are full of their labors. What more can be said? I realized from the outset that this could not be a definitive work. I could not presume to address all that had been said before in Christian history, much less the significant contributions to the theme originating outside of Christianity. My contribution will be limited by my abilities and church tradition.

The commission I received from World Vision's Latin America and Caribbean Regional Office had the following guidelines. The work should:

- not be highly academic;
- avoid, wherever possible, making references and footnotes in the text;
- target a knowledgeable, serious, professional, yet searching audience that is restless, and even dissident, in issues of Christian faith;
- take seriously the daily dialogue about issues of spirituality and mission in Latin America;
- engage in dialogue with contemporary theological movements and influences in the Latin context, such as: fundamentalism, liberationism, Pentecostalism, Anabaptism, Catholicism, constantinianism, evangelicalism and pietism, among others;
- seek an integrated approach, that is, biblical seriousness with an immediate and specific relevance to the context of suffering in Latin America;

- organize the material for study and reflection in small groups, with topics relevant to our Christian walk.

I have tried to incorporate the following components in each reflection:

- a perspective of humility, acknowledging our human limitations in trying to understand God;
- topics related to the principal theme;
- striking chapter titles to stimulate the imagination and to open various perspectives on the theme;
- a question, perspective, saying or proverb as a point of meeting, dialogue and point of departure;
- a number of possible focal points for the issue being dealt with;
- a serious, exegetical, but accessible use of the biblical text, to illuminate the issue to be dealt with;
- some ideas regarding the connection between the specific theme chosen and the general subject of this book, that is, with Christian spirituality and mission; and
- chapters designed to open dialogue not end it, to stimulate reflection not discourage it, to extend, not limit, the horizon.

Some chapters are more difficult than others. The easy writings do not always penetrate as deeply as the reader might wish, and the difficult writings do not always communicate as they should. I hope the reader has the patience to study what seems difficult, and the wisdom to strengthen what appears too simple. I have tried to find a balance between these two options.

The principal thesis of this work is that there is no human experience outside of the realm of the Spirit of God, because all of creation emanates from God. To speak of spirituality is to speak of human experience with God's creation. Hence the parameters for reflection are broad, and I hope that the topics chosen open, not close, the panorama. I do not suggest that this work exhausts the theme's possibilities.

The first chapters, since they define the principal concepts of the work and introduce the basic arguments necessary to under-stand what we will later assume as foundational, need to be read carefully. After these chapters the sequence of the material is less important. The topics may be read consecutively, but it is not essen-tial to do so. Please feel free to search for topics that are of most interest at the time. My hope is that the reader's curiosity and the material's content converge so that the entire text is studied, discussed and understood.

I want to give a heartfelt thanks to the people who were a driving force behind this effort; the visionaries, editors, technical teams, and all those who have supported this project in a special way. Specifically, I want to thank Manfred Grellert (vice president, World Vision Latin America and Caribbean Regional Office); Cèsar Romero (director, World Vision Colombia); Glendon Klaassen (Executive Secretary of the Commission on Overseas Mission in Newton, Kansas); the teams of CLARA (Colombia) and World Vision (Costa Rica and MARC), in matters of editing, revision and publication; my son Derek for translating; my brother Jim for editing the manuscript; and my wife, Irene, and my family for their support and constant stimulus in the project. Last but not least, I thank God for permitting us to have the creative Word as the foundation of our reflection.

Part 1

1

Prologues and preparations

Classical theologians had an interesting tendency in their writings. Often they began their systematic theology with a preface they called a *prolegomenon; pro* is the Greek word indicating something "prior to," while *legein* means "to speak." Thus, a prolegomenon introduces that which is important to say before it is said. This emphasis might seem strange to us: How can you say something before saying it? Haven't you already begun to speak in introducing what you will say?

But this practice made sense. These theologians realized that their underlying assumptions played an essential role in understanding the work. It was, therefore, important to say a few things to introduce what they really wanted to say.

On approaching the subject of Christian spirituality and mission, it struck me more and more that anything a human being might dare to say is really a prolegomenon; that is, it is to speak before truly speaking. Christian spirituality, after all, refers to the work of God's Holy Spirit, the Spirit characterized by freedom and truth. It seems presumptuous to claim to speak in this Spirit's name. The Bible also makes clear that Christian mission is of God. God is the author, the Alpha and Omega, of mission to the world. God has the true word: what we say is a prolegomenon.

It is also presumptuous to claim to speak more than the prolegomenon because of one's perspective. To speak of Christian

3

spirituality and mission presupposes that one is located within this narrative of commitment, discipleship and obedience, that is, within the community of the Spirit. I believe we all feel an immense gap between what we already know about spirituality and mission, and how we practice what we know. We can readily identify with Isaiah when he recognizes God's presence:

> "Holy, holy, holy is the LORD of hosts;
> the whole earth is full of his glory." (Isa. 6:3)

And yet, how easy it is to respond with him:

> "Woe is me! I am lost, for I am a man of unclean lips,
> and I live among a people of unclean lips; yet my eyes
> have seen the King, the LORD of hosts!" (Isa. 6:5)

I ask that you think of this entire book as a prolegomenon, written to prepare us to hear the speech of the free and true Spirit of God communicating with us and with our world.

2

Initial approach

Even what seems most obvious sometimes requires definition. For some, to speak of *spirituality* and *mission* may seem to be the easiest, most obvious and natural thing to do. But let's define what we intend to say with these words.

First, it is important to note that both words, *spirituality* and *mission,* are not Christian words in and of themselves. They are not even always religious words. For example, to speak of the spirit of the times is not a testimony to the religious nature of the speaker, and mission can also refer to goals of a multinational corporation, a government program, or a military effort. The Christian must define these words to avoid confusion with these other common meanings.

Spirituality refers broadly to those ultimate values and commitments that govern our wishes and dreams. It is the framework within which our actions make sense to us. These values and commitments can be otherworldly and nonconformist, but they can also faithfully reflect the secular values of the world around us. Sometimes secular values reflect otherworldly values; that is, they reflect values of the rule of God that one often meets in unexpected places. In this broad sense every human being, institution and human organization—every human structure—has a spirituality that can be recognized and defined. In other words, they are directed toward certain spirits that govern them and provide their reason for being. The author of Ephesians wisely warns:

> For our struggle is not against enemies of blood and flesh, but against the rulers, against the authorities, against the cosmic powers of this present darkness, against the spiritual forces of evil in the heavenly places. (Eph. 6:12)

For a Hebrew, and consequently for the Bible, to speak of spirit is to speak of life. Three Hebrew words can mean spirit: *nefes*, which means "vital spirit"; *ruach*, which means "wind" or "breath of life"; and *nesamah*, which is "breath." Spirit is the strength, creativity, power, abundance, creation and producer of life. Thus, to speak of the Holy Spirit is to speak of the life that God generates.

To speak of Christian spirituality is a double task:

1. to identify the values and commitments that relate to the Spirit of God that are the values of life itself; and,
2. to know and recognize how to differentiate this Spirit from other spirits that demand our loyalty but may be spirits of death.

Christian spirituality, then, refers to the alignment of our human spirit with the Spirit of God.

The word *mission* is especially difficult to speak about from a biblical perspective because it is a post-biblical Latin word, not Greek, Hebrew or Aramaic. And the meaning of the Latin *missus* is a bit slippery, since its meaning changed and was enlarged from medieval to modern Latin. It has two meanings:

1. an assigned task (vocation, calling); and,
2. the act of sending (to send).

The term emerged from the Jesuit world and was initially used to describe the duty of the church as sent to the world. Yet it is also the favorite word used to translate important concepts of the New Testament, thus replacing Greek words that have lost some of their richness in the Latin translation.

In the Great Commission of the fourth Gospel, for example, two Greek words are often translated as mission:

> Jesus said to them again, "Peace be with you. As the Father has sent [apostelo] me, so I send [pempo] you.

. . . Receive the Holy Spirit. If you forgive the sins of
any, they are forgiven them; if you retain the sins of
any, they are retained." (John 20:21–23)

The author relates sending with the apostolic task in this passage; that is, to do mission is to be an apostle. He also emphasizes
the spirituality of the task, since it is through receiving the Holy
Spirit that mission happens. We learn the content of the task and
the sending: it is related to "sin." The mission of the Spirit is to
discern, forgive and retain the "sins" of the world, and as such, it is
the mission of the apostles.

In the Great Commission (Matt. 28:18–20) we see other elements of this mission. We are called to disciple, baptize and teach.
All of this is done in the name (the authority) of the Father, the Son
and the Holy Spirit.

We find even more wealth of meaning when we investigate the
other side of sending—mission as vocation.

I therefore, the prisoner in the Lord, beg you to lead a
life worthy of the calling [klesis] to which you have
been called [kaleo]. (Eph. 4:1)

The root of the Greek noun klesis and the Greek verb kaleo
refers to a vocation, mission, invitation and calling. It is also the root
of the verb parakaleo, which literally means "to invite to the side
of"; that is, to accompany, console, exhort, persuade, beg, help and
advocate. The task of advocating for the other is the mission of the
sent.

The verb parakaleo becomes the noun parakletos, which is
translated as "Advocate" (John 14:16, 26; 16:7). The task is to
"walk alongside of" the needy person, to accompany the person
suffering the effects of sin (whether their own or that of others). The
mission to advocate, to be a voice in favor of the other, is the task of
the Spirit.

And there's more. The root from which the counselor Spirit
grows is also the most common word to speak of the church. The
noun klesis (vocation) combines with the preposition ek (out of), to
form the noun ekklesia (literally, those with the vocation outside of).
That is, the church are those called out, those invited to accompany,

those who have the mission *(klesis)* of the Advocate *(paraklete)*. Thus mission becomes our spirituality, and spirituality becomes our mission.

If we see Christian spirituality as aligning the human spirit with the Spirit of God, we can also see Christian mission as aligning the human task with the task of God. As a result, Christian spirituality and Christian mission are inseparable and virtually synonymous.◟

3

Our way of speaking

It is not easy to speak of the relationship that exists, or should exist, between Christian spirituality and Christian mission.

On the one hand, spirituality is nothing less than the Christian's mission, the alignment of the human spirit with the Spirit of God. On the other hand, mission is nothing other than the spiritualization of all of our human activity, the alignment of human activity with God's activity in the world. For all intents and purposes, spirituality and mission are complementary. Normally the small and inconspicuous word *and* refers to the coexistence of two different parts, but this conjunction does not suggest that these two parts express a common meaning, much less that they are synonymous. So it is not the most appropriate word to describe the relationship between spirituality and mission.

The conjunction *or* usually expresses opposition or contradiction between two parts; it tends to connect two exclusive dimensions. Therefore it is not an appropriate word to link the relationship between Christian spirituality and mission either.

Other prepositions and prepositional phrases that might fulfill this function are *of, in, for, before, without, through, according to, further than, for the purpose of, beneath, within, over, toward, with, beside, after.* Though several of these could serve to emphasize some relationship between spirituality and mission, all of them have something in common: they connect a noun, or an initial idea, to a larger and more important construct, and in themselves negate an egalitarian or synonymous relationship between the two parts. For example, the "spirituality of mission" establishes "mission" as the principal fact and "spirituality" as its subordinate dimension. On the other hand, the "mission of spirituality" subordinates "mission" to "spirituality," and that also negates our principal thesis.

Another possibility would be to use verbs that normally connect a subject and a nominative, though both are nouns. The clearest example is the verb *to be*; for example, "The mother is Mary," or "Mary is the mother." There is no doubt that both nouns, *mother* and *Mary,* refer to the same person. Nonetheless, not all mothers are named Mary, and not all Marys are mothers. If "mother" takes the position of the subject, it means that we know something: she is a mother, and we wish to clarify who she is, "Mary." If "Mary" becomes the subject we know *who* it is, "Mary," and we want to know *what* she is, "mother." However, this usage presupposes prior information or clarity about one of the two nouns, which then becomes the subject. Again, this does not resolve how to speak of spirituality and mission as equal or synonymous.

Nor does it work to reduce one of the two nouns to an adjectival function, as in "missionary spirituality" or "spiritual mission". When changing one of the nouns to function as an adjective the subject subordinates the modifier, and this is not useful to us in the discussion of spirituality and mission.

Both Christian spirituality and mission are like God's Word described in Hebrews,

> living and active, sharper than any two-edged sword, piercing until it divides soul from spirit, joints from marrow; it is able to judge the thoughts and intentions of the heart. (Heb. 4:12)

The struggle to keep spirituality and mission as one is the challenge of this study.

4

The problem of dualism

Clement of Alexandria, in the second century after Christ, wrote this about the fourth Gospel:

> Finally John, who saw that the external [literally, "corporal"] facts had already been clarified in the other Gospels, and being encouraged and pushed by his friends and inspired by the Spirit, composed a spiritual gospel.

Clearly reflected here is the tendency toward dualism in the early church, a tendency undoubtedly influenced by Greek and Gnostic philosophies. Dualism is the separation of human reality into the corporal (material, physical) and the spiritual.

This tendency is still very much with us. We easily speak of the social, economic, political, religious and spiritual today, as if the spiritual were something alien to the social, economic, political and religious. We speak of physical and spiritual bread, as if physical bread were not part of the spiritual agenda. We speak of the physical salvation of the body and the spiritual salvation of the soul. We speak today of sex as corporal activity and prayer as spiritual activity. We speak of giving bread to the hungry as a social ministry and evangelization as a spiritual ministry.

After centuries of living, thinking and acting within this dualistic worldview, it is difficult for us to return to the biblical text in order to search for and understand the integral nature of creation and the essential role of humanity within it. The Hebrew worldview, out of which the biblical text grew, struggles to maintain all things created by God as a spiritual realm, because they are of God, who is Spirit.

The spiritual is not contemplating the essence of things but rather contemplating their origin and, therefore, their purpose and end, since purpose is normally best revealed in origin. Sex, for example, is a spiritual act if it fulfills the purpose of its origin; politics is a spiritual process if it fulfills the purpose of its origin; the distribution of land and bread is spiritual if it fulfills the vision of the origin of land and bread. Of course, these remain spiritual processes even if they do not fulfill the purpose of their origins; but then they fulfill the purpose of spirits that are not of God.

An example from John 3:1–8 (RSV):

> Now there was a man of the Pharisees, named Nicodemus, a ruler of the Jews. This man came to Jesus by night and said to him, "Rabbi, we know that you are a teacher come from God; for no one can do these signs that you do, unless God is with him." Jesus answered him, "Truly, truly, I say to you, unless one is born anew [anothen], he cannot see the kingdom of God." Nicodemus said to him, "How can a man be born when he is old? Can he enter a second time into his mother's womb and be born?" Jesus answered, "Truly, truly, I say to you, unless one is born of water and the Spirit, he cannot enter the kingdom of God. That which is born of the flesh is flesh, and that which is born of the Spirit is spirit. Do not marvel that I said to you, 'You must be born anew' [anothen]. The wind blows where it wills, and you hear the sound of it, but you do not know whence it comes or whither it goes; so it is with every one who is born of the Spirit."

The key word in this passage is *anothen*, and it has two meanings. One is "anew"; it concentrates on the process of birth and was understood thus by Nicodemus. The other meaning is "from above";

it concentrates on the origin, the source of birth, and was thus understood by Jesus. Nicodemus's mistake underscores the real intent of the word: one must be born from above, from God, from the Spirit; one must be born to the purpose of one's origin, one must align oneself with the purpose of God. The flesh is not evil, but if it does not recognize the purpose of its origin then it aligns with another purpose and cannot "enter the kingdom of God." This makes sense. To mistake your origin means to arrive at a different destination.

A Spanish proverb says, "For those who do not know where they come from or where they are going, any bus will do." Christian spirituality and mission is a search for our origins, thereby finding our destinations. We know that there are many "buses" (spirits) that do not originate with God and consequently cannot take us to the destination of divine purpose.

Christian mission that is born "from above" will recognize all that is created by God as spiritual by virtue of its origin in God, in the Spirit. The task of this spiritual mission is to invite creation to reconcile itself once again with its creator, with its origin.

> All this is from God, who reconciled us to himself
> through Christ, and has given us the ministry of rec-
> onciliation. (2 Cor. 5:18)

Christian spirituality that is born "from above" recognizes all of God's creation as its framework for mission, whose task is to invite creation to unite with God and with the presence of God's Spirit in all of creation.

> [God] has made known to us the mystery of his will,
> according to his good pleasure that he set forth in
> Christ, as a plan for the fullness of time, to gather up
> all things in him, things in heaven and things on earth.
> (Eph. 1:9–10)

Both Christian spirituality and mission have two goals:
1. to recognize all of creation as an extension of its origin, God; and,
2. to return all of creation to the purpose of its origin and in this way to reconcile it with its Creator, God.

Wolfhart Pannenberg, a German theologian, says, "Sin is to confuse the source of life in our search for life." That is, to sin means to assign to abundant life a false origin, or not to recognize the real origin (source) of abundant life. We all search for life. Christian mission shows that in recognizing God the creator Spirit as the source of life—that is, in spirituality—all of creation is united both with its origin and destination of abundant life.🌿

Part 2

5

Where are we going?

The Bible begins in Eden and ends in the New Jerusalem. Both the origin and the destination of the biblical witness point toward the same realities:

- harmony among human beings;
- harmony between the human and nature;
- harmony between the human and God;
- harmony between nature and God;
- ecological harmony;
- psychological harmony;
- sexual harmony;
- cultural harmony;
- the abundance of peace;
- the absence of suffering;
- the absence of evils;
- the absence of tears and sadness;
- the purpose is life in abundance.

Some may say, "That's utopia." That could be. But Christian spirituality and mission are concerned with collaborating with God in the reconstruction of these utopias. But more than utopias, they are expressions of origins and destinations.

How can we know if a spirit is of God? By putting it to the test. Where does it lead? Let's consider a modern example from David Ray Griffin.

> We notice the emergence of a new culture in our world:
> a culture which . . . has generated a global crisis. His-
> tory teaches us that it is the first truly global crisis since
> the Ice Age. At that time the danger emerged from
> nature, but now it arises from the hands and minds of
> human beings. (Griffin, 56)

Griffin goes on to cite two dangers in the modern world with
the capacity to destroy the world as we know it: nuclear capabilities
and the ecological devastation of the world. Both are products of
human malice and violence.

If we compare these dangers with the biblical origin in Eden
and the destination in a New Jerusalem, it is not difficult to see that
these threats do not reflect this origin nor are they en route to this
destination. We can be certain that these realities do not emerge
from the Spirit of God but originate in spirits that are not of God.
Christian spirituality and mission emerge from ecological, human
and divine harmony, and move toward abundant life. Many modern
spirits have other origins and move toward destruction, violence and
death.

Thus nuclear issues and the ecological destruction of the world
are, in a profound sense, spiritual issues, matters for Christian spirituality and mission. To align oneself with the Spirit of God and with
the divine activity in God's creation also means to oppose the spirits
of violence and evil that drive us toward ecological and nuclear destruction.

The apostle Paul said, "The last enemy to be destroyed is death"
(1 Cor. 15:26).

German theologian Jürgen Moltmann writes:

> If Paul says that death is the "last enemy," then the
> contrary is also true: that the resurrected Christ and
> the hope of the resurrection are enemies of death and
> enemies of whatever world [spirit] that generates and
> promotes death. (Moltmann, 21)

To promote and generate death, as nuclear warfare and ecological destruction do, goes against Christian spirituality and mission. It arises from other spirits.

To make this discernment meaningful, we must identify and name the modern spirits that drive us toward destruction, to make them recognizable. It is not easy, and of course, our list is not exhaustive, but we can point out some of the modern spirits that seduce the world with promises of happiness.

Some elements of modern non-Christian spirituality are[1]:

Individualism

All that is required is for oneself to be oneself. (Descartes)

Dualism

Once we can isolate the human soul from its relationship to the body and nature, only then can we ideologically justify the domination and exploitation of nature, physical violence and ecological destruction. This drive to dominate, master and control is one of the more central characteristics of modern non-Christian spirituality. Also, relegating God (as supreme representative of divinity and holiness) to heaven and emphasizing transcendence while denying divine immanence (presence) within God's creation allow modern spiritualities to abuse creation, without "sinning" against the Creator.

Futurism

The tendency to search for the meaning of the present solely in the future, with no consideration for the past, is futurism.

Secularism

Secularism does not imply a decrease of religiosity, but a transfer of religious devotion to objects or ideologies that do not transcend the world, but rather gain fulfillment within the world itself. This religious fervor can express itself in fascism, communism, capitalism, nationalism, scientism, estheticism, nuclearism, narcissism and so on.

Nihilism

Nihilism is to deny the "ultimate" in life, negating the possibility that objectivity or normative value can exist.

---

[1] The following list has been compiled from various sources, including David Ray Griffin, *Spirituality and Society*, and Harry Huebner and David Schroeder, *Church as Parable*.

Relativism

All value judgements are relative to the circumstances of the case. There is no objective way to declare one thing better than another. Ultimate values can only be achieved through nonrational decisions. One can decide in favor of nationalism and against Christianity, but there is no rational basis to declare one better than the other.

Determinism

Everything happens as it should. Determinism is a fatalism that denies the possibility that human decisions can affect the direction of history. It is demonstrated by sayings such as "If God is willing," and "No one dies before his time."

Scientism or positivism

One can only arrive at truths through the scientific method, because it is not concerned with the issue of values. Other disciplines such as theology, ethics and metaphysics can never assert an objective truth.

Self-interest

Especially evident in the economic arena, the only adequate basis for decision-making is self-interest.

Narcissistic personality

Immediate self-gratification is the only ethical criterion. This personality rejects responsibility for the future and for others in today's society.

Mechanization (technologization, industrialization, specialization, bureaucratization)

Social organization that accommodates the worker to the machine, rather than the machine (or system) to the worker.

Materialism

The primacy of economics and "things" over human social relationships.

The psychologizing of morality

> We do not speak of character but of personality.
> We do not speak of right or wrong but of values.
> We do not speak of convictions but of feelings.
> We do not speak of guilt but of shame.

The politicizing of morality

> Public opinion, majority feeling and democracy are worth more than ethics or morality.

> We do not value people for who they are, but for what they produce.

> Legality replaces morality.
> Rights replace responsibilities.

Although one can find positive values in some of these spirits, there is no doubt that, on the whole, these modern spirits walk behind, beside and ahead of human experience, leading and pushing us toward destruction. The constant and continuous task of Christian spirituality and mission is to discover and discern how and where these spirits align with the Spirit of God, and how and where they oppose God's Spirit.

6

Spirituality as a sense of the beyond

You might agree that what has been said up to this point is fine.

Christian spirituality means to align the human spirit with the Spirit of God.

Christian mission means to align human activity with divine activity.

Christian spirituality and mission are inseparable, even synonymous.

We need to avoid dualism in our understanding of creation.

We need to understand spirituality as a recognition of our real origin.

We need to understand mission as a return to this origin of life.

But isn't there anything more? you ask. I'd always understood that

Mission is done; spirituality is felt.

Mission is to act; spirituality is to be.

Mission is to agitate; spirituality is to calm down.

Mission is visible; spirituality is invisible.

Mission is external; spirituality is internal.

Mission is communitarian; spirituality is individual.

Mission appeals to the mind; spirituality appeals to the heart.

Mission is to participate in the known; spirituality is to give oneself to mystery.

Mission is to express oneself; spirituality is to listen.

Mission is natural; spirituality is supernatural.

Mission is ethics; spirituality is hope.

Isn't spirituality expressed most clearly in moments of worship, when I feel the Lord at my side?

song, when I raise my hands to the sky?

prayer, when I feel a voice that answers me?

ecstasy, when the Spirit allows me to speak in the Spirit's tongue?

the laying on of hands, when I feel divine warmth in my soul?

prophecy, when I know that God is being revealed?

healing, when the power of God is manifest?

spiritual warfare, when I see demonic powers being crushed?

miracles, when I see the fulfillment of God's promise?

temptation, when I feel the power to resist?

testing, when I feel the power to persevere?

frustration, when I feel the consolation of God?

joy, when the happiness of the Lord surrounds me?

A parable from Anthony de Mello, a Catholic priest, states:

A man traveled halfway around the world to see for himself the extraordinary fame that the Teacher enjoyed.

"What miracles has your Teacher performed?" he asked one disciple.

"Well, actually . . . there are miracles and there are miracles. In your country they consider it a miracle if God does someone's will. We consider it a miracle when someone does the will of God."

This parable shows the double-sided nature of spirituality and mission:

- to be receptive and sensitive to what God does for us; and,
- to be obedient to the will of God in our lives.

Both things can be miracles; they are supernatural acts.

The two-sided exhortation to cultivate spiritual sensitivity and to be obedient is also found in the prophets' exhortations:

> He has told you, O mortal, what is good;
>> and what does the LORD require of you
> but to do justice, and to love kindness,
>> and to walk humbly with your God? (Mic. 6:8)

Jesus also refers to this double-sided nature of spirituality and mission in his summary of the Christian duty:

> "'You shall love the Lord your God with all your heart, and with all your soul, and with all your mind.' This is the greatest and first commandment. And a second is like it: 'You shall love your neighbor as yourself.' On these two commandments hang all the law and the prophets." (Matt. 22:37–40)

There is a spiritual world beyond our understanding, because God is spirit, and our knowledge of God will always be limited. And there is a visible and palpable spiritual world, near to us, because God the Spirit has created a universe in which God has left witnesses, with spiritual presence, in creation. Christian spirituality and mission involve opening ourselves to respond to this spiritual presence of God.

7

Criteria for spiritual discernment

✿

In the most literal sense to speak of that which is *spiritual* simply means to recognize that there is something beyond human comprehension and control. The spiritual affirms a sphere of reality beyond the human one. As we have already said, *spirit* and *spirituality* are not Christian concepts in themselves, although they are often religious concepts. Many religions believe in a spiritual realm beyond human control. Even secular ideologies recognize a world beyond human control. Witchcraft, satanic sects, Buddhism and Hinduism also affirm a world of spirits, that is, a spiritual world. Marxists, sometimes called materialists, speak of structural or systemic influence over people who live under or within these structures and systems. This is one way of affirming the reality of powers beyond our understanding. For Christians, the spiritual also points to a world beyond ourselves.

I want to emphasize the multifaceted reality of spirituality, since many in our churches relax when they hear someone speak of spirituality, thinking that this person is therefore one of us, a brother or sister in Christ. It is not so. As Christians we are among many who affirm a spiritual dimension of human existence.

I am reminded of an experience I had in Bolivia. We went to a wedding in a mining town far from the city, at a high altitude and in a cold climate. The townspeople did not have many luxuries, but it seemed as though everyone had a television set. They told us that every Sunday at 9 A.M. everyone watched the program of a North American evangelist; they even had to postpone local worship services until after the program.

"What a man of God," many told me. "He can preach, sing, cry and pray all at the same time."

"And what about his message?" I asked. "Is it a sound, biblical message?"

"*Caramba*, we don't know," they replied. "We've never really paid much attention to the message."

It is understandable, then, to question how we distinguish between Christian spirituality and the presence of spirits that are not Christian. New Testament writers are also concerned with this problem, and teach us that discerning spirits is an important task of the Christian walk.

Paul says:

> Do not be conformed to this world, but be transformed by the renewing of your minds, so that you may discern what is the will of God—what is good and acceptable and perfect. (Rom. 12:2)

We could also accurately transcribe, "Do not be conformed to the spirit of this world," or, "Do not be conformed to the spirituality of this world." And we notice that this is a task made possible only by a "renewed understanding" that has transformed us. To understand the spirit of God means to distance oneself from other spirits that seek our loyalty.

Paul also says:

> And this is my prayer, that your love may overflow more and more with knowledge and full insight to help you to determine what is best, so that in the day of Christ you may be pure and blameless, having produced the harvest of righteousness that comes through Jesus Christ for the glory and praise of God. (Phil. 1:9–11)

Here is another call to insight and to knowledge. But this time Paul gives us some ways to recognize the spirits that are of God:
- they direct us toward justice (righteousness);

- they are measured against the person of Jesus Christ; and,
- they do not contradict the praise and glory reserved for God.

These are significant clues for our task of discernment.

John the Elder says:

> Beloved, do not believe every spirit, but test the spirits
> to see whether they are from God; for many false
> prophets have gone out into the world. (1 John 4:1)

Not only does John say that there are spirits that are not of God, but also that these spirits are incarnated in false prophets. One does not search for spirits by looking into the air but by listening to the messages of the preachers and the prophets. In other words, each spirit has its messengers and our task is to listen carefully so as not to be deceived.

John continues:

> By this you know the Spirit of God: every spirit that
> confesses that Jesus Christ has come in the flesh is
> from God, and every spirit that does not confess Jesus
> is not from God. (1 John 4:2–3a)

According to John, the principal criterion to discern correctly the spirit of God is "Jesus Christ in the flesh"; that is, the historical Jesus, the Jesus who ministered in Palestine, the Jesus who ate with the poor and purified the temple and the Jesus who suffered instead of resisting. The priest, prophet, king, teacher Jesus is the fundamental criterion to measure whether or not a spirit is of God. We could say that the Holy Spirit has flesh. It is not a matter of guesswork, but of confidence in the person of Jesus of Nazareth.

The Elder continues:

> And every spirit that does not confess Jesus is not
> from God. And this is the spirit of the antichrist, of
> which you have heard that it is coming; and now it is
> already in the world. (1 John 4:3)

Was the Antichrist already in the world when the Elder wrote in the first century? How is that possible? Won't the Antichrist come just before Jesus' second coming? Look carefully: the Antichrist is someone whose life or message does not reflect the spirit of Jesus. This is why the discernment of spirits is so important; we must not become Antichrists.

Again, the Elder states:

> Children, it is the last hour! As you have heard that antichrist is coming, so now many antichrists have come. From this we know that it is the last hour. They went out from us, but they did not belong to us; for if they had belonged to us, they would have remained with us. But by going out they made it plain that none of them belongs to us. (1 John 2:18–19)

The plot thickens! There wasn't only one Antichrist but many! Not only were they not in the air, they were "among us!" They did not come from somewhere else but from us! To what is the Elder referring? It appears that the Elder's community divided, and the division was due to some in the congregation who denied the importance of the historical Jesus as the foundation of faith.

> Who is the liar but the one who denies that Jesus is the Christ? This is the antichrist, the one who denies the Father and the Son. No one who denies the Son has the Father; everyone who confesses the Son has the Father also. (1 John 2:22–23)

The Christian spirit, the Spirit of God, the Holy Spirit, has parameters: it must align itself with Jesus. If not, it is another spirit.

To bring the issue down to earth: the principal means of recognizing the Holy Spirit's presence is all that is characterized by Jesus' presence in the world. The compassion, mercy, justice, forgiveness, love, service, joy, peace, kindness, communion, faith and gentleness that characterize the person of Jesus are also sure signs of the presence of the Christian spirit (see Gal. 5:22–25). It is not speaking in tongues or experiencing a certain feeling, emotion or miracle that is the principal measure of the presence of Christian spirituality but rather the alignment of our character and action with those of Jesus.

8

The holy, the sacred and the consecrated

To speak of holiness in our context is to speak of moral purity; to speak of the sacred is to speak of divine perfection; to speak of the consecrated is to speak of human commitment to divine perfection, the cleansing of sins. Although these definitions have their strengths, we despair before them. Despite every possible effort we soon notice, if we are honest and transparent (also characteristics of the purity we seek), that we are neither pure nor clean nor perfect. If our understanding of spirituality is defined only by perfection and purity, by an existence without stains, then we cannot experience a valid spirituality. To be relevant to who we are, human spirituality must contemplate imperfection, a lack of purity and sins.

When we look at the biblical text, we find that the priests and prophets speak of the sacred and the holy with a somewhat different meaning. They define holiness as a characteristic of God. And the most pronounced characteristic of the holiness of God is God's transcendence, the difference of God, the separation of God from everything else, that which is distinctive about God. In other words, the Bible speaks of the sacred and holy primarily as something that distinguishes the Creator from creation, something that separates the Creator from creatures, something that by definition exists beyond human comprehension.

The prophet Samuel says:

> There is no Holy One like the LORD,
>   no one besides you;
>   there is no Rock like our God. . . .
> for the LORD is a God of knowledge. (1 Sam. 2:2, 3)

The writer of Exodus asks:

> "Who is like you, O LORD, among the gods?
>   Who is like you, majestic in holiness,
>   awesome in splendor, doing wonders?" (Exod.
>   15:11)

The answer to these rhetorical questions is: no one. There is no holiness like that of God; there is no rock like God; there is no one who is like God; there is no majesty like that of God; no one deserves praise like God; no one is as awesome as God. God is different, distinct and other. The Bible even identifies the human effort to become God as the original sin, the Fall. Eating the fruit in the Garden of Eden and constructing the Tower of Babel are two examples by which human beings wanted to reach heaven, to emerge from their human condition and become God (see Genesis 3 and 11).

Otto, a German theologian, has identified five themes the Bible develops to insist upon the otherness of God.

1. The greatness of God: the abundance of power that is in God; a power so incredible as to evoke within us fear of God's wrath.
2. The majesty of God: the abundance of the being of God; a being so different that no one can approach God; a presence that repulses the presence of everyone else.
3. The energy of God: the urgency, vitality, power, emotion and activity that manifests itself with the presence of God as a fire in our midst.
4. The mystery of God: the transcendence, that which is distinctive, supernatural, the incomprehension that God's presence generates.
5. That which is fascinating about God: the fascination, en-

chantment, intoxication, adoration and exaltation that flow from the mere presence of God.

We can see these characteristics in Exodus 19, one of the many passages on which these concepts are based:

1. "The whole mountain shook violently (v. 18); . . . and God would answer [Moses] in thunder (v. 19) . . . 'Go down and warn the people . . . or the LORD will break out against them'" (v. 21–22).

2. "Be careful not to go up the mountain or to touch the edge of it. Any who touch the mountain shall be put to death (v. 12). . . . Otherwise many of them will perish (v. 21) . . . The people are not permitted to come up to Mount Sinai" (v. 23).

3. "Now Mount Sinai was wrapped in smoke, because the LORD had descended upon it in fire" (v. 18).

4. "I am going to come to you in a dense cloud, in order that the people may hear when I speak with you and so trust you ever after" (v. 9).

5. "But do not let either the priests or the people break through to come up to the LORD" (v. 24).

But something of the mystery, energy, power, incomprehensibility, obscurity, majesty and enchantment of God is accessible to human beings. In biblical language, glory represents that which God reveals so that humans can respond to the divine presence. The glory *(shekinah)* of God is all aspects of God that we can touch, see and understand. This is the great message of Christianity:

> And the Word became flesh and lived among us, and
> we have seen his glory, the glory as of a father's only
> son. (John 1:14)

And, there is something of the mystery, energy, power, incomprehensibility, obscurity, majesty and enchantment of God that is repeatable in human beings. The divine element that we can repeat is by the grace of God. It is through grace that God's glory is recognized. It is through grace that this glory can be understood and applied to human behavior. We often call this application of divine glory in our context the mission of the people of God. It is this people's duty to pay attention to what is revealed of God's being (glory) and to apply it to our context (mission). By the grace of God, we can speak of holiness as a human quality as well. We also call this search for the glory of God spirituality, and its application, mission. Nonetheless, the glory of God that we find, and are able to apply in our lives, will always remain an incomplete accomplishment: God continues to be God, we continue to be human. To err in this basic reality is to deviate from the spiritual path that God has laid out for us.

The priests and prophets of the Old Testament sought to keep people alert, ready to recognize the glory of God whenever and wherever it manifested itself. The principal purposes of the writings, laws, prayers and observation of holy days and times (such as the sabbath, sabbatical year and jubilee) were to reflect the glory of God and to remain alert in order to recognize more of God's glory whenever God would be manifested even more. The tabernacle and the ark of the covenant, and later the temple, were places of encounter with the glory of God. The Torah was a visible expression of the manifestation (glory) of God for and with God's people.

> There once was a disciple who asked her Teacher: "What can I do to ensure God's coming?" "There is nothing that can be done," answered the Teacher. "Then what good are the spiritual disciplines—prayer, meditation and fasting?" questioned the disciple. "These disciplines keep us awake so that when God does arrive we don't miss it," said the Teacher.

This story from Anthony de Mello captures, more or less, what I have tried to say. The holiness of God is of God. By grace God shows us something of this holiness, and this is called God's glory. We cannot do anything to deserve or guarantee this grace and this glory. By putting into practice what we already know about God, we remain alert to recognize more when God reveals more. Remaining alert through inquiry and practice is what we call Christian spirituality and mission.

9

What about justice?

❦

Among some in Latin America there is a feeling that saints are not preoccupied with issues of justice, and that those who struggle for justice are not dedicated to holiness (sainthood). We now want to look briefly at several passages to discern the connection between holiness and justice in the Bible.

Text:

> The LORD is king; let the peoples tremble!
>> He sits enthroned upon the cherubim; let the earth
>>> quake!
> The LORD is great in Zion;
>> he is exalted over all the peoples.
> Let them praise your great and awesome name.
>> Holy is he! (Ps. 99:1–3)

Comment:

The psalm begins with God as "other": greatness, majesty, power, transcendence, exaltedness.

Text:

> Mighty King, lover of justice,
>> you have established equity;
> you have executed justice

and righteousness in Jacob.
Extol the LORD our God;
   worship at his footstool.
   Holy is he! (Ps. 99:4–5)

Comment:

The holiness of God has been expressed through the love of justice, establishing equity and exercising justice and righteousness. These are attributes that lead us toward exaltation.

Text:

Moses and Aaron were among his priests,
   Samuel also was among those who called on his
      name.
   They cried to the LORD, and he answered them.
He spoke to them in the pillar of cloud;
   they kept his decrees,
   and the statutes that he gave them.
O LORD our God, you answered them;
   you were a forgiving God to them,
   but an avenger of their wrongdoings.
Extol the LORD our God,
   and worship at his holy mountain;
   for the LORD our God is holy. (Ps. 99:6–9)

Comment:

Despite God's holiness, God responded to human beings. It was not the purity nor the perfection of Aaron, Moses or Samuel, but the character of God as one who forgives. God was manifested to God's servants, maintaining the holiness of the divine (in the pillar of cloud).

In summary, Psalm 99 demonstrates that the holiness of God expresses itself in righteous equity, and justice toward God's people. God is revealed as a lover of justice. The only adequate response of God's servants was that "they kept his testimonies, and the statutes that he gave them." That is, the holiness of God manifests itself in justice, and God's people respond by keeping and exercising this same justice as a faithful reflection of the holiness of their God. Justice is evidence of the glory (the revealed holiness) of God. The holiness of God translates into acts of justice realized by God's servants who have remained sensitive to the manifestation of God's holiness. That is, holiness becomes real through the spiritual sensitivity of its servants. This sensitivity (spirituality) can do nothing other than also manifest itself in works of justice (mission).

Let's look at another example, which may seem slightly more complicated but is also very revealing. A part of the Ten Commandments that caused a great deal of discussion among the people was this:

> For I the LORD your God am a jealous God, punishing children for the iniquity of parents, to the third and fourth generation of those who reject me, but showing steadfast love to the thousandth generation of those who love me and keep my commandments. (Exod. 20:5–6)

This commandment is repeated when Moses encounters God on the mountain (Exod. 34:6–7). Upon hearing these words, Moses

> quickly bowed his head toward the earth, and worshiped. He said, "If now I have found favor in your sight, O Lord, I pray, let the Lord go with us. Although this is a stiff-necked people, pardon our iniquity and our sin, and take us for your inheritance." (Exod. 34:8–9)

This was a discussion regarding individual responsibility before the commandments of God: how are we affected by the sins or the faith of our ancestors? This text says that God will punish the sins and reward the faithfulness of parents for many generations. Moses begs for mercy and forgiveness. A refrain emerges from this discussion that is later cited in Ezekiel:

> The parents have eaten sour grapes, and the children's teeth are set on edge. (Ezek. 18:2)

But the Lord says:

> As I live . . . this proverb shall no more be used by you in Israel. (Ezek. 18:3)

The entire chapter then argues that God will reward each person according to his or her path, regardless of what the person's parents did before. If the parents were just, but the children were not, the children would perish and the parents would live. If the parents were unjust and the children repented, the children would live and the parents would die.

> Cast away from you all the transgressions that you have committed against me, and get yourselves a new heart and a new spirit! Why will you die, O house of Israel? For I have no pleasure in the death of anyone, says the Lord GOD. Turn, then, and live. (Ezek. 18:31–32)

What interests us is the new list of actions that guarantee the life of the people:

> If a man is righteous and does what is lawful and right— if he does not eat upon the mountains or lift up his eyes to the idols of the house of Israel, does not defile his neighbor's wife or approach a woman during her menstrual period, does not oppress any one, but restores to the debtor his pledge, commits no robbery, gives his bread to the hungry and covers the naked with a garment, does not take advance or accrued interest, withholds his hand from iniquity, executes true justice between contending parties, follows my statutes, and is careful to observe my ordinances, acting faithfully—such a one is righteous; he shall surely live, says the Lord GOD (Ezek. 18:5–9)

That which begins in the heart of the holy, untouchable God who has "no pleasure in the death of any one" ends with the guarantee of life for anyone who repents: "He is righteous; he shall surely live." Morality and ethics become instruments of the holiness of God. The spiritual sensitivity of the human being changes the direction of history through its mission. The repentant person can reveal the glory of God to the needy world. This person participates in the construction of life, which has been God's objective since creation.

Justice and righteousness, equity and reconciliation, are manifestations of the holiness of God that are channeled through the people. Once again we see that the spirituality and mission of God should not be separated in human beings.

Although the given example appears somewhat confusing, do not be discouraged. Once in a while the Bible gives us a brief, clear summary that is easy to understand. Thank God, we have a summary that clarifies all that has been said above:

> He has told you, O mortal, what is good;
>> and what does the LORD require of you
> but to do justice, and to love kindness,
>> and to walk humbly with your God? (Mic. 6:8)

The holiness of God is revealed in the spirituality of God's people. The mission of this people proclaims the holiness of God. The spirituality and mission of God's people are inseparable.🍂

Part 3

10

Spiritual gifts: Subordinating the spiritual to the functional?

In Paul's writings we find many signs of the Holy Spirit's presence in the life of the Christian community. He describes this presence as the manifestation of spiritual gifts (1 Cor. 12:1; 14:1,12), the seal of the Holy Spirit (Eph. 4:30), the measure of Christ (Eph. 4:7) or the fruits of the Spirit (Gal. 5:22). These are different ways to say the same thing: we are the benefactors of God's Spirit working in our lives.

There is a long list of how the Spirit makes itself known in the community:

words of wisdom
words of knowledge
faith
healing
miracles
prophecy
help
administration
discernment of spirits
speaking in tongues
interpretation of tongues
apostles

prophets

evangelists

pastors

teachers

But even more interesting, this array of gifts also has well-defined parameters. Let's look at some of these:

"for the common good" (1 Cor. 12:7)

"that there may be no dissension within the body" (1 Cor. 12:25)

"the members may have the same care for one another" (1 Cor. 12:25)

the gifts have to be clothed in love (1 Cor. 13)

to speak for "upbuilding and encouragement and consolation" (1 Cor. 14:3)

to "build up the church" (1 Cor. 14:4, 5)

"strive to excel in [spiritual gifts] for building up the church" (1 Cor. 14:12)

it is not good when another is not edified by our gift (1 Cor. 14:17)

"that person will bow down before God and worship him, declaring, 'God is really among you'" (1 Cor. 14:25)

"let all things be done for building up" (1 Cor. 14:26)

"so that all may learn and all be encouraged" (1 Cor. 14:31)

"but all things should be done decently and in order" (1 Cor. 14:40)

"to maintain the unity of the Spirit in the bond of peace" (Eph. 4:3)

"for building up the body of Christ" (Eph. 4:12)

"speaking the truth in love" (Eph. 4:15)

"building itself up in love" (Eph. 4:16)

In other words, although it may seem contradictory, even the Spirit of freedom is firmly subjugated and tied to God's intent for creation. Many other characteristics can help us recognize the Spirit's presence: if an activity does not show love, does not edify, does not take the community seriously, if it is individualistic or insensitive to the needs of others, then it simply cannot be of God. The spiritual is subordinated to the functional. That which is spiritual does not exist in the air or in the clouds; it is in life, in hands and feet, in speech and listening, in administration and preaching, in teaching and in analysis, in denouncing and announcing, in reason and unity. Spirituality is shown not only in emotions, feelings, praise, fasting and prayer, but also in obedience, perseverance, commitment, faithfulness and discipleship.

Let's look at an example from the Bible: the Galatian church. This church had a serious problem. In his letter to these Christians, Paul says he is "astonished" because they are separating themselves from the gospel that he had preached to them, and are following another gospel (1:6–9). And it seems that some in the church are questioning Paul's authority to teach, since he was never an apostle of Jesus (1:10—2:10). The church was influenced by "Judaizers," people who taught that the Gentiles had to keep Jewish law (2:11—3:29). In the midst of these fights, Paul reminds his readers of the importance of unity in Christ and of the gifts that Christ gave to the community (4:1–31). He calls them to remain firm in the freedom of the Spirit and to separate themselves from the fruit of the flesh (5:1–26).

We are especially interested in what it means to be spiritual in this example. Paul says:

> If we live by the Spirit, let us also walk by the Spirit.
> Let us have no self-conceit, no provoking of one another, no envy of one another. Brethren, if a man is overtaken in any trespass, you who are spiritual . . .
> (Gal. 5:25–6:1, RSV)

Before moving on, let's take careful note of what Paul is saying. In the midst of the problems the church is experiencing, the people should not forget how to approach such situations spiritually. The spirituality of those who claim to have the Spirit must manifest itself concretely. Let's see what it means to be spiritual in this case. In Galatians 6, I find six signs of spirituality in Paul's teaching:

1. "Restore such a one in a spirit of gentleness. Take care that you yourselves are not tempted" (6:1b).
2. "Bear one another's burdens, and in this way you will fulfill the law of Christ" (6:2).
3. "All must test their own work" (6:4).
4. "Those who are taught the word must share in all good things with their teacher" (6:6).

5. "You reap whatever you sow" (6:7).
6. "So let us not grow weary in doing what is right, for we will reap at harvest time, if we do not give up" (6:9).

How interesting! Spiritual maturity is measured by the effort made to restore the fallen ones (and we all know that this is not easy); the ability of self-analysis; the strength to bear burdens that someone else places upon the community; interacting intelligently with the teacher (whoever teaches); learning the lesson of the harvest (what we reap, we will sow); and perseverance in difficult times. This is how someone who is spiritual behaves. Spirituality becomes functional. Spirituality affects one's temperament, strategy, ethics and hope. Mission is accomplished within this spiritual framework. Finally, it is not difficult to find Jesus' example in these six points; he fulfilled them all.

To live "the law of Christ" like this is true freedom:

> For freedom Christ has set us free. Stand firm, therefore, . . . (Gal. 5:1a)

11

The fundamental work of the Spirit: The creation of the community

W hat is the fundamental work of the Spirit of God upon which all other work is based? Surely most of us would say, with good reason, that it is impossible to rank the many works of the Spirit. Nonetheless, each of us would have an answer. Let's reflect on some of the answers that, in effect, are present in our churches.

Some say that the most important, or the most spiritual, are:
- the gift of tongues
- the power to perform miracles
- the blessing of internal well-being
- the voice of liberation (in its many forms)
- the mystery of prophecy
- the discernment to interpret prophecy and tongues
- the manifestation of truth
- the witness of holiness (sainthood)
- perseverance in prayer and fasting
- the patience to suffer
- the courage to struggle
- the conviction to evangelize
- the wisdom to teach

And the debate will continue. Anthony de Mello tells this story:

> On a certain occasion the Teacher asked his disciples
> what they believed was more important: wisdom or

> action. The disciples responded unanimously: "Action,
> of course. What good is wisdom if it is not expressed
> through action?" "And what good is action if it pro-
> ceeds from an ignorant heart?" responded the Teacher.

This debate about ranking the works of the Spirit is behind
denominational differences, doctrinal conflicts and even the social
strategies of churches and modern movements. Here is a partial list
of such groups:

Pentecostals
Charismatics
Liberationists
Fundamentalists
Anabaptists
Pietists
Catholics
Sectarians
Evangelicals
Guerrilla movements

Let's look at this debate using three biblical paradigms that
relate new beginnings for the Spirit of God: creation, the ministry of
Jesus and the beginning of the church.

First paradigm
Both the Greek word and the Hebrew word for Holy Spirit have the
double meaning of spirit and wind.

> In the beginning God created the heavens and the
> earth. The earth was without form and void, and dark-
> ness was upon the face of the deep; and the Spirit
> [wind] of God was moving over the face of the waters.
> (Gen. 1:1–2, RSV)

Creation was without form; there was a void; there was darkness. This is the world in any age we examine. Disorder, emptiness,
darkness: there is no better way to speak of modern human experience. It's a perfect description.

God's Spirit comes with the intention of addressing the situation. God's mission is to generate life out of formlessness and dark-

ness. The solution to the problem begins. And what is the solution's climax? It is the creation of *adam*: the *adam* in the image of God the creator, male and female (Gen. 1:27). *Adam* means "human being," and it is used to refer to the creation of the couple. This social entity, this communal nucleus, culminates creation, God's first effort to bring meaning to the empty world, the disorder and the darkness.

Genesis 2 continues the same emphasis. Creation is not complete until there is the *adam*, male and female, in its social-communal relationship. The Spirit's solution to human alienation was the creation of the family, the communal nucleus, which complements the social-communal nature of humanity. The most important work of the Spirit of God is to create the community of the Spirit.

Second paradigm

Although Luke the evangelist shows the Holy Spirit as very active before, during and after the birth of Jesus, we will limit ourselves to looking at the activity of the Spirit in the definition of Jesus' mission.

The temptations of Jesus were a struggle to define his purpose. It is a hermeneutical struggle, in which the devil quotes the Bible (Isa. 42:1; Pss. 2:7; 91:11–12), and Jesus responds with other passages (Deut. 8:3; 6:16; 6:13—see Matt. 4:1–11). The dispute is about how to read the Old Testament so that the will of God can emerge, for both the Messiah and the community that the Messiah will form. Will this community provide strategies for how to govern the nations, or strategies for the miraculous intervention of God's army, or economic strategies for the production and distribution of bread? The answer is given indirectly by saying that these proposals are of the devil; that is, they are satanic proposals.

Jesus rejects these temptations immediately after his baptism, during which "the heavens were opened to him and he saw the Spirit of God descending like a dove and alighting on him" (Matt. 3:16). The discernment necessary in the desert was possible through the spirituality of Jesus: the presence of the Spirit of God in his life.

After having received the Spirit of God, and after having discerned the right (and the wrong) path by means of a more sound hermeneutical approach, Jesus is ready to begin his mission. And what is his first plan of action? He establishes a community of disciples, the twelve (Matt. 4:18–22). This is a community that represents the will and strategy of the Spirit of God to resolve the chaos,

disorder and emptiness in the world. Once again, the most important work of the Spirit of God is to create the community of the
Spirit.

Third paradigm

Jesus dies; the disciples become discouraged. Jesus is resurrected;
the disciples awaken. Jesus leaves; the disciples wait "gazing up toward heaven" (Acts 1:10). The disciples go to Jerusalem. The Day
of Pentecost, the coming of the Holy Spirit, arrives, and what happens?

In Acts 2, there are three elements in particular that remind us
of the experience of God's people in the Old Testament:

1. The strong wind

Clearly this reminds us of the wind of the Exodus, where the
wind of God opens a path through the Red Sea, so that a people of
the wind could be born—a people who would walk into the desert,
accept the law of God and make a communal covenant with the
God of their liberation. This event is remembered through the Day
of Pentecost, representing a new Exodus from this temporal
kingdom's enslavement, a new people of a New Covenant.

2. The fire of God's presence

The pillar of fire that guided the people in the desert, in the
book of Exodus, returns on this occasion as tongues of fire that
"rested on each of them" (Acts 2:3). The Holy Spirit, the essence of
the fire, touched each person to form a community of the Spirit.

3. Hearing their own tongues

The miracle of tongues in Acts 2 is not so much the miracle of
speaking different languages, but the miracle of being heard:

> . . . each one heard them speaking in the native lan-
> guage of each. Amazed and astonished, they asked,
> "Are not all these who are speaking Galileans? And
> how is it that we hear, each of us, in our own native
> language?" (Acts 2:6b–8)

This happening reminds us of an opposite event: the confusion of languages during the Tower of Babel's construction in Genesis. There, the community was divided because of its members'
desire to leave behind their responsibility as humans before the cre-

ator God; here, by again accepting its covenant in the Spirit of God, the divine will is heard in every language. The important difference is the Spirit of God. In other words, once more the Spirit creates a community of the Spirit: it returns the human community to the purpose of its origin in God.

What is the primary work of the Spirit of God? I believe that it is the formation of a community that walks in the world with the power and presence of the Spirit. The Holy Spirit creates community; modern spirits create individualism. All the other gifts of the Spirit—prophecy, miracles, healing, liberation or tongues—have their reason for being as expressions of the community of the Holy Spirit. Modern spirits discerned in previous chapters go against this priority of the formation of Christian community as the vehicle and voice of the Holy Spirit in the world.

Christian spirituality and mission emerge from this sense of community, are nourished in community and push for the formation of communities guided by the Holy Spirit. All other objectives of spirituality and mission are subject to this general purpose.

12

The folly of a Christian spirituality of the Cross

〰

> For the message about the cross is foolishness to those who are perishing, but to us who are being saved it is the power of God. For it is written,
> "I will destroy the wisdom of the wise,
> and the discernment of the discerning I will thwart."
> (1 Cor. 1:18–19)

These words from Paul may lead some in our modern context to relax and think: This passage doesn't apply to me, since I'm neither wise nor clever. It sure is letting intellectuals have it!

Who can deny that there is an anti-intellectual, anti-philosophical, anti-educational reflex in our churches, often backed by these words from Paul? But let's take another look at what Paul says in the first chapters of 1 Corinthians.

Paul does not speak against the importance of wisdom. He says divine things are so profound that they can only be understood with the help of the Spirit of God (2:11–12).

Second, although the thoughts of God are profound, God has not left us without help. God has given us "the Spirit that is from God, so that we may understand the gifts bestowed on us by God" (2:12).

Third, it is our vocation, our calling, to understand this divine wisdom (the word *klesis* [call], discussed in chapter 2, is now used in 1 Cor. 1:26: "Consider your own call . . . "). And the purpose of this vocation is revolutionary. Paul says it is "to reduce to nothing things that are" (1:28). This wisdom is so deep, says Paul, that we must interpret spiritual truths with spiritual means (2:13), and that will seem foolishness to someone who does not have this Spirit (2:14). The wisdom of this world also appears foolish when seen through the eyes of the Spirit (3:18–19).

What started this discussion between Paul and the Corinthians? It was something very human. There were fights, contentions and divisions within the community itself. Its members had forgotten their "foundation" in Jesus Christ (3:11). They were divided; some were following Peter, others Apollos and others Paul (1:10–13; 3:3–9).

Let us reflect further on this idea that the message of the Cross is folly, and that the wisdom of the world rejects this message as foolishness. If the Cross is absurd, then what is the alternative? Where will we find wisdom? What are the criteria to discern wisdom? Why is it necessary to understand the Cross from the perspective of the Spirit of God in order for the Cross not to seem foolish? What is there in the wisdom of this world that opposes God's lesson on the cross? These are not easy questions, but we will try to get a step closer to some answers.

The Cross always has to do with how to address sin in the world through the divine love of God. As Christians we say that through the death of Jesus (the Cross) our sins are forgiven. Paul says:

> God proves his love for us in that while we still were
> sinners Christ died for us. (Rom. 5:8)

Perhaps this understanding helps us to comprehend the wisdom of this world.

How does this world address the issue of sin? If addressing sin through the route of the Cross seems crazy, what is the alternative the world provides?

Paul suggests the answer. The Cross is foolish for the world because it

- is a demonstration of human weakness
- does not have power
- makes us losers instead of winners
- makes us victims, not conquerors
- kills us instead of giving us life
- asks for the enemy's forgiveness instead of seeking revenge
- implies giving ourselves up instead of defending ourselves
- proposes surrender instead of going to war
- proposes a loyalty that supersedes nationalism
- spills the blood of the innocent instead of the blood of the guilty
- does not respond in kind against initiators of violence
- does not respond to death with death but with a prayer of life
- does not react to another's sin with sin

In summary, to the world the Cross is folly because it hands back historical and human destiny to the hands of God. And this, for our world, is crazy. For those of us who prefer to eat the fruit of Eden and construct the Tower of Babel, it is folly.

The world's answer for addressing sin is more power—to win, conquer, kill, seek revenge, defend itself, fight, love self, establish national boundaries, kill the guilty. The world's answer is violence, death and more sin.

In other words, the wisdom of the world does not have faith that God can and wants to resurrect, that God asks for our obedience, and that God will be responsible for the resurrections that assure abundant life. The wisdom of the world prefers to assume total responsibility for the historical project, using the strategies of sin to be victorious over sin.

The proclamation of the Cross is indeed crazy in that context. And the wisdom of the world is folly for the Cross.

> And we speak of these things in words not taught by human wisdom but taught by the Spirit, interpreting spiritual things to those who are spiritual.
>
> Those who are unspiritual do not receive the gifts of God's Spirit, for they are foolishness to them, and they are unable to understand them because they are spiritually discerned. (1 Cor. 2:13–14)

Martin Heidegger, philosopher and theologian, writes:

> The thing that makes us think the most and that demands profound spiritual thought and discernment in our time, is that we still aren't thinking. (Bailie, 256)

I believe that Paul would paraphrase Heidegger thus:

> The thing that makes us think the most and that demands profound spiritual thought and discernment in our time is that we still are not thinking spiritually about how to address sin in the world.

13

The gospel of mission, the mission of the gospel

❦

Is it possible to be precise about the mission of the gospel?

Is it possible to find the nucleus of the gospel that provides the foundation for our mission?

Some will say that the nucleus of the gospel is salvation by faith. Others will say that this nucleus is faith by grace. Still others, that it is faith that works justice. And still others will say that it is the incarnation of the divine presence in everyday life.

Let's go to the beginning of Jesus' ministry to investigate more closely an answer to these important questions.

> Now after John was arrested, Jesus came into Galilee, preaching the gospel of God, and saying, "The time is fulfilled, and the kingdom of God is at hand; repent, and believe in the gospel." (Mark 1:14–15, RSV)

It is important to note that the word *gospel* appears twice in this short passage. Jesus preaches or announces the gospel, and the gospel demands repentance and belief. But what does the word *gospel* mean?

In Greek, this word is made up of two parts: *eu*, which is the Greek way to express something beneficial, good, positive; and *aggelion*, the Greek word meaning "message," "announcement" or "news." It has the same root as the word *angel,* which means "messenger" or "one who brings a message."

Euaggelion means welcome news, a positive message, a beneficial announcement, a good proclamation. But the word itself does not indicate the content of this good message; it does not say what this good news is. The text just tells us that Jesus brought a good message from the desert to Galilee, and that it was a positive message of God.

Looking at the text more closely, we see that the good message Jesus brings contains two elements: (1) the time is fulfilled; and, (2) the kingdom of God is at hand.

The good message is precise, brief and clear: in God's time the power (rule) of God has made itself known in Galilee.

The power of God is revealing itself! What great news for those who align themselves with God! What dangerous news for those who oppose the reign of God! For this to be a good message, the listeners must come and align themselves with the platform of the power that is revealing itself. If the listeners prefer that the power of God stay far away, this announcement is bad news.

Why would this be good news? For whom would this be a good message? Under what circumstances would this news be welcome? These questions are not answered in this passage, although a clue is left: it will be a good message (gospel) for those who respond to this act of power with repentance and faith.

Just as the message is composed of two elements, so two elements are required as part of the listeners' response: (1) repentance (*metanoia*, in Greek); and, (2) faith (*pistis*, in Greek).

Metanoia means "radical change"—a whole transformation, a complete about-face; *pistis* means "confidence," "trust."

The message that God's power was revealing itself in Galilee was a question of seeing things from a different perspective; of renewing one's worldview; of trusting that one could find the will and power of God in the events that were going to happen in and through Jesus Christ; and of entrusting the direction of history and one's life to this new power.

Some time ago I saw a young woman with a T-shirt that read:

> Since thinking cannot guide us to a new way of living,
> the new way of living will guide us to a new way of
> thinking.

This saying deals with the same elements as Jesus' announcement: the relationship between transformation and faith. According to this T-shirt, only transformation can guide us to a new worldview. It is impossible, the shirt claims, for transformation to occur through a change of thinking.

Although the message may seem similar, I do not believe that this is what Jesus announces in the passage. The impetus for metamorphosis can come from either thought or repentance. We cannot separate the two. I know people, intellectuals, who through lessons, study, discussion and logic have arrived at repentance, changed their lives, committed themselves to a new lifestyle and taken seriously the presence of God's kingdom in their lives. On the other hand, I also know people who have had a new experience in life—perhaps they were tortured or visited a poor country for the first time—and this experience changed their lives. The relationship between repentance and faith is mutual, dynamic and integral. To mention these two elements as Jesus does is not a matter of sequence, that repentance must precede faith. But it proves their inseparable nature. That is, one cannot change a lifestyle without changing one's faith, and one cannot change faith without changing one's lifestyle.

The content of Jesus' message is clear. The gospel means:

- We must align our lives with the presence of the kingdom of God in the world.
- The heart of the gospel is the coming of God's kingdom in Jesus Christ.
- To proclaim the gospel is to announce that it is possible to live in this world according to the values of God's kingdom.
- Christian mission is to live the kingdom of God.
- Christian spirituality is to open ourselves to God's reign in our lives.
- Christian mission and spirituality have the same origin and the same destination: the presence of God's kingdom in this world and in our life.
- The firstfruit of the kingdom in the world is when the church faithfully lives and proclaims this good news.

This passage does not say everything. It does not specify, for example, what constitutes the kingdom of God. It does not give us a road map for repentance. It does not point out the path to faith. It simply states that the presence of God's power in the world requires a response, demands an answer. It is impossible to remain neutral before this presence; no answer is an answer in itself. Silence is denial. By not responding we proclaim ourselves indifferent to the announcement. Not paying attention to the announcement implies that we align ourselves with other kingdoms that demand our loyalty. We value this announcement by responding positively to it.

To understand how to live within the presence of God's kingdom in this world is a lifelong challenge. In a sense, it is the only Christian task.

The evangelist Mark makes another important point in this short passage: that this announcement is a message from the outside. We see this emphasis in two ways: (1) the text says that it is a message of God; and, (2) the passage states that the messenger came from the desert to Galilee in order to give the message.

I believe that Mark organizes his material in this way to say something important. The gospel
- comes from the outside
- comes from God
- enters the new context as a foreigner
- has a missionary characteristic
- arrives out of context, or decontextualized, as foreigner/ missionary
- does not completely accommodate itself to any context
- brings a new perspective to the culture
- is not completely at home in any culture
- brings a new worldview, a new language, new definitions, new communal sentiments
- defies routine, and opens new horizons
- asks for the repentance and faith of the host culture

At first glance this seems to go against the modern emphasis on contextualization of the gospel to each new culture, era and generation. It also seems to contradict some modern concepts that emphasize the divine in each culture: that each culture has its own Old Testament, that what is important is to embody the gospel in each culture, that for the gospel to be relevant we must contextualize it to the modern era, and that the gospel loses its relevance by not being indigenized.

But it is not a contradiction.

These emphases make sense and have the same starting point: the naked gospel does not fit into any culture; it requires contextualization. Nonetheless, it is different.

Instead of basing contextualization on similarities that exist between the gospel and the host culture, I suggest it is important not to deny or hide the differences, the points of divergence between the gospel and the host culture.

Clearly the gospel must be relevant to every culture; if it were not, it would not be gospel. If the gospel is not relevant to my situation, it is not good news for me. But what makes the message relevant is precisely the fact that the gospel is different. It is capable of injecting new options into the same old answers; it can offer new alternatives to those that have already been tried. By being foreigner/missionary, the gospel can propose and introduce new directions, untried approaches, untraveled paths and unexplored processes.

It is precisely this foreigner/missionary characteristic of the gospel that makes it the Good News of God, that makes this message from the desert relevant for everyone. It is this characteristic that makes the gospel a message with truly beneficial possibilities.

Part 4

14

The spirit of sex, sex of the Spirit: Sex as a public act

The seminary where I taught in Cochabamba, Bolivia, invited theologian Peter Savage to teach a continuing-education course to church pastors and leaders, mostly men. Dr. Savage began one session with this question: "When are you more spiritual: when you are in bed with your wife, or when you are in church praying?"

Though relevant, in the Aymara/Quechua/evangelical context this was a jarring question. Isn't the answer obvious? Does sex have anything to do with the Spirit? Does spirituality involve sex?

At another seminary, in Bogotá, Colombia, where I was teaching a course in Christian ethics, I asked students to suggest a topic of special interest since the course outline was flexible. Unanimously they asked me to lecture on Christian sexual ethics. I did, and one woman dared to comment: "You, brother, are from another planet. No one here has ever thought like that."

Despite these experiences, I again dare to approach the topic of the spirituality of sex. I do it with the support of the apostle Paul who, surprisingly enough, classifies sex as a gift of God, literally, a *charisma* of God. In the same letter in which he gives a detailed outline of the Christian duty with regard to spiritual gifts (1 Cor. 12—14), Paul includes sexuality as a spiritual gift (1 Cor. 7:7).

It is no surprise that Paul applies exactly the same criteria to this gift of the Spirit as to the others. He subordinates the spiritual gift of sex to what is edifying: "one having one kind and another a different kind" (1 Cor. 7:7c). Let's look more closely at the argument and logic of 1 Corinthians 7.

1. Sexuality is also included within the framework of the mission of God: what counts is "obeying the commandments of God" (7:19). "I say this for your own benefit, not to lay any restraint upon you, but to promote good order and unhindered devotion to the Lord" (7:35).

2. The Christian community can consider options that are radical in its context, for example, the option to remain single (7:25-26). Neither Paul's Jewish culture nor the Corinthians' Greek culture permitted a young woman to remain outside masculine authority. A "loose" woman was considered a target for fornication. The fact that Paul considers singleness an option for women shows the trust and responsibility he gave to the body of Christ, to the community that will "bear one another's burdens, and in this way you will fulfill the law of Christ" (Gal. 6:2).

3. We can be very flexible in discerning sexual practice because it is not the most important issue. Paul speaks of a "concession" (7:6). If you do one thing, it's all right; if you do the opposite, that's fine too, but "do not sin" (7:27–28,36). If you have the gift of self-control, don't get married; if not, marry (7:8–9, 36–38). Thus, sexuality is also defined as existing within the overarching framework of the community obedient to the mission of God.

4. In 1 Corinthians 7 it is obvious that sex is to be practiced within the bonds of commitment and marriage. It is important for us to reflect on this issue, which still causes great debate today. Why should sexual activity occur exclusively within the bonds of marriage? Paul gives some preliminary reasons:
   - within marriage there is mutual subordination, wife to husband and husband to wife (7:1–5);
   - within marriage there is a mutual dedication that desires the other's well-being (7:5); and
   - within marriage there is long-term commitment (7:10–16).

But behind these considerations lies another issue that has to do with the authority to be married. Sometimes we automatically think of the act of matrimony as a legal act we perform before a judge to legalize our marriage in the eyes of the State. Sometimes we ask: Does the State determine the commitment I have to my spouse? Is not my commitment with God and my spouse? Isn't that enough?

I believe Paul would say yes and no. When Paul speaks of marriage he does not refer to acknowledgment by the State but the authorization of the community, the body of Christ, for the faith commitment between two of its members. In other words, Paul teaches that sex is practiced within the public authorization of the body of Christ. Why? Because as stated above, the community sees marriage as mutual subordination, as mutual dedication and as long-term commitment. The community also recognizes the problems and possibilities of being single and is willing to support the person if this is his or her decision.

Said in another way, the sexual act is a public act, not in the sense that it should be practiced in the church sanctuary, but in the sense that it is practiced with the blessing and authorization of the Christian community. Why a public act? Because this act is so intimately tied to the spirituality of people, and the spirituality of a Christian is a public issue. There is no spiritual sphere that is strictly private, hidden or individual.

I do not believe that Paul had a legalistic obsession in linking sex to marriage; it is, rather, a question of the integral character of human/Christian existence. How could one leave something as important as a couple's sexual relationship out of its spiritual context? To do so would be schizophrenic; it would divide the integrity of human existence in an artificial and superficial way.

To answer Peter Savage's question: What one does in bed with a spouse is done openly, knowing that the Spirit, as delegate of the community, is in the bed as well. If it isn't good for the Spirit to see what I do, it isn't good to do. If it isn't good that the community finds out what I do and with whom I do it, it isn't good to do. The sexual act, within the framework of the authorization of Christ's body, is not shameful; it is a celebrative and joyful act, enjoying what God has created in us and recognizing that this gift has also been discerned, blessed and authorized by our sisters and brothers.

This is a double-edged sword. It does not just consider the spirituality of the sexual act; it affirms that the sexual act is also a spiritual act. In other words, the same criteria of spirituality mentioned previously apply to this act. Sex is not a world separate from the life of the Spirit. It, too, must be practiced within the framework of justice, compassion, service, dedication, commitment, community, obedience and discipleship.

15

The spirit of money, the money of the Spirit: Financial management

❦

Money? Is this also an issue of spirituality? Is there a spirit of money that is more Christian than another? Does the Spirit manage finances, budgets, interest, debts, taxes? Doesn't anything exist outside of the spiritual sphere? Sex, and now money?

The key question is: What are the parameters for spiritual money management? Let's look at several concrete cases.

The apostle Paul organized an offering among the Greek churches for the mother church in Jerusalem. It seems that the Jerusalem church was in economic difficulties, and Paul saw this as a challenge not only to help the church, but also to use the offering as a metaphor for the reconciliation of two peoples, Jews and Gentiles. Let's look at 2 Corinthians 8-9, to find some clues to the spirituality of money.

Paul gets our attention by using the word *thanks/grace* (*xaris*) ten times in these two chapters. Grace demonstrates the holiness of God. God allows us to understand something of Godself; God reveals something of God's holiness. What we can understand of God's revealed holiness (glory) is by divine grace. For those who take advantage of it, this revelation demonstrates God's generosity toward us. Grace produces a profound gratitude within us, because the God of the universe has been revealed like this. Thus, we direct our gratitude toward the grace of this holy God.

God revealed Godself willingly, freely and generously. These characteristics of the manifest holiness of God also form the foundation for our holiness (spirituality). First, grace (xaris) is what God reveals to us:

- "to know . . . about the grace of God that has been granted"(8:1); and
- to recognize "a fair balance between your present abundance and their need" (8:14).

This divine grace also generates an attitude of thankfulness in us:

- "Thanks (xaris) be to God" (8:16); and
- "Thanks be to God for his indescribable gift" (9:15).

By the grace of God this gratitude pushes us to perform gracious acts toward others:

- to show the grace (xaris) to participate in helping the saints (8:4);
- to complete this gracious (xaris) work among you (8:6);
- to provide in abundance for every good work (9:8) . . . that through us will produce thanksgiving to God (9:11);
- to overflow in many thanksgivings to God (9:12); and
- To act for the glory of the Lord and to show our goodwill (generosity) (8:19).

And since faith, speech, knowledge and love form part of our spirituality, we are to "excel in this gracious work also" (8:7, RSV).

Once again the lesson of the harvest is used: "The one who sows sparingly will also reap sparingly, and the one who sows bountifully will also reap bountifully (9:6).

But Paul gives other foundations for a spirituality of money:

- the church in Macedonia begged to have the opportunity to give. Giving is not an obligation but a blessing (8:4);
- to give and to help is a response made from within tribulation, poverty and joy, and not outside of them (8:2);
- this joy meant that the church gave beyond its means (8:3);
- the church took the initiative to give, "not only to do something but even to desire to do something" (8:10);
- "for if the eagerness is there" (8:12), give according to what you have, not according to what you do not have (8:12);
- the offering is "proof of your love" (8:24); it is voluntary, "not an extortion" (9:5);

- the offering "supplies the needs of the saints" (9:12); and brings the beneficiaries to praise (9:13–14).

Two remaining motives deserve special emphasis:

- "I do not mean that there should be relief for others and pressure on you, but . . . a fair balance" (8:13–14); and
- "I am testing the genuineness of your love" (8:8).

These last two motives are important: love searches for ways to be genuine. Spiritual love is not satisfied with a feeling of well-being toward everyone but searches for ways to put this feeling into practice. One criterion in the search for efficacy is "that there may be a fair balance" (8:14).

How important this appeal is for the global body of Christ! These days we often classify the relationship between churches in North America and churches in Latin America as the universal body, global family and as partners in mission. But we continue to construct churches costing millions of dollars in the North and churches of hardened mud (adobe) in the South. We continue to spend millions of dollars on educational resources for children of the North, and use materials that are out of context and employ poor pedagogy for children of the South. This is neither a question of relief nor of frugality, but a question of "fair balance." Fair balance does not yet exist in the Christian family.

Allow me to share an experience of spiritual money management. A poor church I know in Latin America noticed that, despite having plenty of money, its partner church in North America was spending less and less on ministries of justice, peace and social issues, and more and more on infrastructure (buildings, air conditioning and furniture). Instead of asking for more from its partner church, the poor one collected an offering and sent it north, specifically designated to help in the social ministry of its church partner. It was a humble offering of US$250, but extremely significant. This situation was not a question of relief but of equality. It was an important witness that had a strong spiritual impact on the northern church. This was a concrete way of making the bond of love between the two bodies genuine.

The spirituality of the Year of Jubilee

Jesus links the character of his ministry to the Year of Jubilee found in the Old Testament. Recall the characteristics of Jubilee in Leviticus 25:10–41:

- to proclaim liberty to all inhabitants of the land;
- to return each to the ancestral home;

- not to cheat anyone;
- not to sell land in perpetuity (because it is God's);
- not to charge interest or sell food for profit;
- to forgive debts so the debtor can be freed; and
- to fallow the land.

The Year of Jubilee is the institutionalization of equality, liberty and productivity, that is, social justice for the people of God. If for some unforeseeable reason some become rich and others become poor and enslaved, Jubilee guarantees that these inequalities will not be perpetuated, but that a fresh start, a new opportunity, will come every fifty years. In other words, poverty, injustice and inequality must not become institutionalized within the society or community. Structural and systemic sins are minimized. Social injustice cannot feel comfortable within these social systems and structures.

Echoes of Jubilee recur in the teaching and worldview of Jesus.

- The admonition not to worry about what we will eat or drink (Matt. 6:25–34) reminds us of the land's rest, during which time God will provide;
- Jesus' announcement in the synagogue of Nazareth (Luke 4:18–19) faithfully reflects the concepts of Jubilee: good news to the poor, release to the captives, sight to the blind, freedom for the oppressed, and the arrival of the year of the Lord's favor;
- The model prayer of our Lord (Matt. 6:9–13) is a prayer of Jubilee with its references to bread, earth, liberation from evil, and forgiveness of debts as we forgive our debtors;
- The parable of the wise steward (Luke 16:1–9) tells of the rich man's praise for the steward who forgave the debts of the common folk;
- The parable of the unforgiving servant (Matt. 18:23–35) reflects the curse of not forgiving debts after one's own have been pardoned;
- "Sell your possessions and give alms" (Luke 12:33) goes beyond offering from earnings to freeing ourselves of our capital to help others.
- The Beatitudes (Matt. 5:3–10) remind us of the themes of Jubilee: the poor, those who mourn, the hungry, consolation, inheriting the earth, mercy and woe to the rich;
- Jesus' teaching regarding loans—"If you lend to those from whom you hope to receive, what credit is that to you? Even sinners lend to sinners, to receive as much again" (Luke 6:34)—

reminds us that creditors did not want to lend close to the Year of Jubilee for fear of losing their money. In Luke 6:35, Jesus exhorts us to lend and expect nothing in return, for it is God who rewards.

Jesus also places economic issues within the parameters of the holiness of God. The intent of the Jubilee Year reveals something of God's holiness. The people responded to this revealed holiness with the institution of Jubilee: a holy management of goods.

The early church also took the spirituality of Jubilee seriously in its financial management:

> All who believed were together and had all things in common; they would sell their possessions and goods and distribute the proceeds to all, as any had need. Day by day, as they spent much time together in the temple, they broke bread at home and ate their food with glad and generous hearts. (Acts 2:44–46)

> No one claimed private ownership of any possessions, but everything they owned was held in common. . . . There was not a needy person among them, for as many as owned lands or houses sold them and brought the proceeds of what was sold. They laid it at the apostles' feet, and it was distributed to each as any had need. (Acts 4:32b, 34–35)

> We see that taking an offering in the churches to help the Jerusalem church was a logical extension of the spirituality of money taught by Jesus and practiced by the early church. The Spirit does provide a foundation for financial management, for the attitudes involved as well as for strategies that make our love genuine. Our management of goods continues to be a spiritual issue. In looking at the issue of money management in our churches today, we cannot deny that we are still affected by some spirit within our context. However, we must ask ourselves: Is this the influence of the Holy Spirit? Or does the influence emanate from a different source?

16

The spirit of power, the power of the Spirit: Human organization in light of Christian spirituality

Let's go right to the heart of the debate about power. There are those who insist that the chief difference between Christian discipleship and party politics is that Christianity is content with weakness while party politics seeks power. They are, quite simply, wrong. The difference is not weakness versus power, but power versus power. What kind of power is truly powerful? What power has the power of radical change? And, what is mistaken?

There are those who propose that the Christian church should distance itself from issues of power. They should never read Paul's letter to the Ephesians!

And there are those who believe that the Christian church should surrender itself to the arbitrary power of the State. They too should not consider the letter to the Ephesians as part of their Bible.

Why is Ephesians so provocative? Let's look at Ephesians 1:17–22:

> I pray that the God of our Lord Jesus Christ, the Father of glory, may give you a spirit of wisdom and revelation as you come to know him, so that, with the eyes of your heart enlightened, you may know what is the hope to which he has called [klesis] you, what are the riches of his glorious inheritance among the saints, and what is the immeasurable greatness of his power for us who believe, according to the working of his great power. God put this power to work in Christ when he raised him from the dead and seated him at his right hand in the heavenly places, far above all rule and authority and power and dominion, and above every name that is named, not only in this age but also in the age to come. And he has put all things under his feet and has made him the head over all things for the church.

"Heavenly places" does not simply refer to another world. It is Paul's way to go to the source, since all of the spirits that operate in this world have their source in different places. Both the power of the church and the power of the powers originate in "heavenly places."

The "mystery" (1:9; 3:3–5, 9) that is given to the church as the heart of its message to the principalities and powers is the message of the social reconciliation of two enemies, Jews and Gentiles:

> that is, the Gentiles have become fellow heirs, members of the same body, and sharers in the promise in Christ Jesus through the gospel. (3:6)

> For he is our peace; in his flesh he has made both groups into one. . . . He has abolished the law . . . that he might create in himself one new humanity in place of two, thus making peace, and might reconcile both groups to God in one body through the cross, thus putting to death that hostility through it. (2:14a, 15–16)

This message of power does not end here. The letter concludes with a strong call to use this power:

> Finally, be strong in the Lord and in the strength of
> his power. Put on the whole armor of God . . . (6:10–
> 11a)

This "armor" is truth, righteousness (justice), the gospel of peace, faith, salvation, the Word of God, prayer in the Spirit, perseverance and the courage to proclaim (6:13–20).

It is so armed that we can face the principalities, authorities, world rulers of this present darkness and spiritual hosts of wickedness (6:12).

The church is irrevocably called to exercise power. But how is the church to exercise this power? This is where we enter the world of the upside-down kingdom. The Bible uses many metaphors, images and symbols to demonstrate the seeming contradiction of exercising true power. The power of the Spirit is released when:

- the seed dies
- we become like children
- we turn the other cheek to one who strikes us
- we give our shirt as well when asked for our coat
- we walk two miles when we are obliged to walk one
- we love our enemies instead of killing them
- we are persecuted for doing justice
- we are so honest that it is not necessary to take an oath
- we do not seek our own honor
- we remove the "log" from our own eye
- we purify the temple
- we break the sabbath for compassionate reasons
- we do not fast just because everyone else is
- we fast when others are celebrating
- we pray in the desert
- we clothe the naked
- we visit those in prison
- we give water to the thirsty
- we give food to the hungry
- we obey God rather than people
- we visit the sick
- we take the path of the cross
- we bless instead of curse
- we suffer for what is good
- we lead as servants, not dictators

- everyone's gifts are used in the congregation
- social barriers lose importance and stop being obstacles
- equality exists between woman and man, husband and wife, slave and free, children and parents
- we share, instead of insisting on our own
- we denounce, like Stephen
- we proclaim, like John the Baptist
- we leave weapons behind, like Moses

The spirituality of power has direct implications for both the internal organization of the church and for its external witness. Internally, the teachings regarding spiritual gifts make it impossible to justify despotic structures within the church as biblical (see Eph. 4; 1 Cor. 12, 13, 14; 1 Pet. 5; Rom. 12). Upon studying these passages and teachings, one immediately notes certain characteristics.

The diversity of spiritual gifts

Diversity allows neither a hierarchy of gifts nor hierarchic leadership. All gifts are important, and all people are equal. All gifts are necessary; all are valid; all cooperate as in a symphony; all are linked as ligaments of the body. None takes the place of another; the eye cannot listen and the ear cannot speak. The gift that becomes most important in a Christian community is the one that is not present, because without it the body is crippled. The nose is not a bad eye; it is not an eye. We do not punish the eye for not being articulate; it is not its function to speak well but to see well. The diversity of spiritual gifts allows us to function as a body. Differences in gifts are reasons to celebrate, not to fight; to cooperate, not to impose; to share leadership, not to isolate; to include people in the ministries of the church, not to exclude them.

The universality of spiritual gifts

Every Christian has at least one gift. The task of the church is to discern each person's gift, encourage its use, give it a place to flourish and celebrate its emergence. In terms of church organization, this means we must not organize ourselves in such a way that some gifts do not fit. It means we must not organize ourselves around only certain people or certain gifts. It means the organization itself should reflect equal access for each one's gift.

The multiplicity of spiritual gifts

A person may have more than one gift. It's not necessarily true that the pastor cannot sing or the administrator cannot preach. It's not necessarily true that one who serves cannot be served, or that one who gives is not needy. It's not necessarily true that only the pastor can counsel or that only deacons can visit. The same person can do more than one thing. This affirmation has direct implications for the structure of the body of Christ. The structure must not confuse the office with the gift; it must not ignore the gift's function in order to focus exclusively on the person's title. Church organization should encourage the use of all gifts of the Spirit for the benefit of the body.

The duplication of spiritual gifts

The same gift may be present in many people. There may be five people with pastoral gifts in the church, or there may be four counselors. The opportunity for everyone's gifts to function optimally continues to be the goal of the body.

The unity of spiritual gifts

Spiritual gifts share the same origin and move toward the same destination. Unity of gifts not only allows for the discernment of gifts in someone but also allows for the discernment of a gift that someone lacks. This second discernment process is no more negative than the first. To say, "Brother, this does not seem to be your gift," is as valid as saying, "Sister, thank God for the gift you are exercising." Unity of gifts does not insist that everyone should do the same thing, but that everyone should exercise the gift(s) he or she has.

When all spiritual gifts are fully exercised, in all of their diversity, multiplicity, universality, duplication and unity, then spiritual power is released, the power of the Holy Spirit the world so badly needs. To release the power of the Spirit in this way is the mission of the church. This is why we are here.

Revelation of this spiritual power also has direct implications for the external mission of the body. When we seek justice, God's power is present. When we administer according to the Spirit of God, when we denounce and announce according to the Spirit of God, when we organize ourselves according to the Spirit of God, when we love each other and our enemies according to the Spirit of God, then, inevitably, we confront the principalities, powers, authorities and rulers of this world who act according to other spirits. This confrontation is the true spiritual battle—a collision of values that shows itself in human organizations and tasks. This spiritual battle is a witness of power to the world. The church proclaims that this is the way true, world-transforming power is realized.🕊

17

The spirit of violence, the nonviolence of the Spirit: Social responsibility

❦

The power of the spirits of this world is ultimately supported by coercion, torture and the threat of death. In the eyes of the world, no power exists over and above these elements. For this reason, weapons legitimate uses of power in the world's eyes, whether civil and military. Might makes right, the saying goes. The hand that controls the armies is in charge. This premise reveals itself at all levels of human organization. Fist fights, capital punishment and obligatory military service all express the prevalence of this respect for violent power. It is part of what produces suffering in our world.

Does Christian spirituality have something to say about this exercise of power? Does Christian mission have anything to do with the presence of these giants in our midst?

Let's look at an important passage in the New Testament.

> [God] canceled the bond which stood against us . . .
> This he set aside, nailing it to the cross. He disarmed
> the principalities and powers and made a public ex-
> ample of them, triumphing over them in him. (Col.
> 2:14–15, RSV)

Something important happened on the cross! The bond (the law) was nailed to the cross; the principalities and powers were disarmed, shown up publicly and utterly defeated on the cross.

How interesting! Wasn't it exactly the opposite? Weren't the principalities and powers the ones who nailed Jesus to the cross? Wasn't it precisely the law, and its interpretation, that won the day? Wasn't Jesus the one who was disarmed, stripped, tortured, utterly defeated and crucified? Weren't the civil, religious and military authorities the winners, the conquerors? Wasn't it Jesus, and through him the power of God, who were utterly defeated?

This passage inverts what seems to have happened: the victim was the victor, and the abuser was utterly defeated; the crucified one was the conqueror, and the murderer was conquered; the corpse was clothed, and authority was stripped; the crucified one was the observer, and the Roman State was the spectacle; the suffering one was right, and the religious authority ridiculed; the nonviolent one was the hero, and the violent one the villain.

What was the core of the controversy revealed in the Cross? None other than the use and abuse of power. The most powerful weapons of the Roman State were torture and death; the most powerful weapons of God are nonviolence and life. The Cross shows that the power of God goes beyond the most powerful weapons of the State. Death had to surrender to life. And ever since then, when the power of life confronts the power of death, we know beforehand who will emerge victorious. The power of death has been disarmed, the strength of torture soundly defeated. There is no greater power than that of the crucified God: the power of life. This is the folly of the Cross.

An argument is often made regarding the "social responsibility" of the citizen, for Christian and non-Christian alike. We say that, although unfortunate, this social responsibility obligates us to use violence in many forms: for discipline in the home, in social struggles, in the military and for national security. The Cross proposes a different option: it shows us that our social responsibility is in our obedience to a powerful God. We can do nothing more socially responsible than to obey God and, by so doing, releasing God's immense power. The power of life will prevail. Life will triumph over the powers of death. Through obedience, we will generate other resurrections.

Paul says something surprising in Colossians:

> I am now rejoicing in my sufferings for your sake, and
> in my flesh I am completing what is lacking in Christ's
> afflictions for the sake of his body, that is, the church.
> (Col. 1:24)

And in Philippians, Paul says:

> For he has graciously granted you the privilege not
> only of believing in Christ, but of suffering for him as
> well—since you are having the same struggle that you
> saw I had and now hear that I still have. (Phil. 1:29–
> 30)

Something was lacking in Christ's afflictions? Our suffering, in some sense, completes what is lacking in Christ's suffering? Heretical! Did you know that these verses were in the Bible? We don't hear many sermons about them. Nonetheless, the meaning is clear: As Christians we can expect the same fate as Jesus; as Christians we can expect that the principalities and powers will also align against us; as Christians we will also need to opt for obedience to God. This obedience, even the cross that may result from it, is our true social responsibility. This is how divine power makes itself present in the world, and we remember that the ultimate weapon of God is the power of life. Although the seed dies, life emerges anew in God.

Christian spirituality and mission, then, present in themselves a social and a political option to the world. It is not true that the church has no response to the politics of the world. That response is to teach the world, through its actions, how to understand the will of God in each concrete situation. We can offer no greater or more relevant gift to the world than the spirituality and mission of the church. This is our social responsibility.❧

18

The spirit of politics, the politics of the Spirit

W e have focused on the fact that Christian spirituality and mission are inseparable, and that both are inextricably linked to ethics, discipleship and ministry, that is, with the Christian walk.

But what about politics? Did Jesus present a political option to his people? Did the movement Jesus began also represent a political alternative for society? These are important questions we need to investigate carefully.

Let's begin with Jesus' answer to Pilate, a response that continues to raise storms of controversy in discussions regarding the political relevance of Jesus for our world:

> Pilate answered, "Am I a Jew? Your own nation and the chief priests have handed you over to me; what have you done?" Jesus answered, "My kingship is not of this world; if my kingship were of this world, my servants would fight, that I might not be handed over to the Jews; but my kingship is not from the world." (John 18:35–36, RSV)

After reading this passage, a reader might say, as many have, "Well, that's resolved! Jesus' kingdom is spiritual and has nothing to do with the dirty politics of this world. It is speaking about heaven, not about earth."

But let's look at Jesus' response more closely. He argues that if his kingship were of this world, his followers would have fought for him not to be handed over. Here Jesus identifies a real political option: the Jewish zealot option would have been to fight. But Jesus' option was *not* to fight and, inevitably, to be handed over. It is a political alternative and brings almost immediate consequences.

Jesus' reason for why his followers did not fight, however, is what leads to misunderstanding. What was the spirituality behind the decision not to fight? Jesus does not give much of an explanation, but he says enough. Twice he states that his kingdom is "not of this world."

It is one small word, *of* in English, *ek* in Greek, that causes such misunderstanding. Many have said that *of* means the location of something. Since the kingdom is not of this world, it must be located in another realm, in the heavenly realm. This means that Jesus is speaking about life after death—heaven—and that he is more concerned with what lies beyond. His kingdom has nothing to do with the political kingdoms of this world. So while we are here, we must commit ourselves to the options of the politicians of this world.

The problem with this answer is that the Greek word *ek* does not mean location. First, *ek* indicates the origin of something, as when someone says, "She is a citizen of Canada." Origin is not necessarily the same as location; a Canadian can just as easily be in the United States. And we have already noted that origin also implies something of purpose. For example, a Canadian's purpose for being in the United States, if he is Olympic gold-medal sprinter Donovan Bailey, would not simply be for pleasure but to win a race against opponents from the United States. In this case origin says a lot about purpose.

Second, *ek* refers to something's essence; that is, the material from which something is made. An example is saying, "This table is made of wood." In this context *ek* describes the characteristics of something, not its location. The table could be made of wood but be in a brick house.

So what Jesus *really* says in his answer to Pilate is this: My kingdom does not originate in this world, nor is its essence characteristic of this world. My kingdom has a different origin and therefore has different values. Since my kingdom is based on a different spirit, it does not obey the spirits that govern kingdoms that originate in and exhibit characteristics of this world.

Despite having a different source and different values, however, his kingdom is *located* in this world. Indeed, it is precisely because of this location in the midst of other kingdoms that it represents a political option for this world, over against the politics of other kingdoms.

Is it possible to be more precise about Jesus' political option? Let's begin with his answer to Pilate.

Pilate says he is not a Jew. Jesus understands perfectly well that Pilate represents the Roman presence in Jerusalem. Nonetheless, Pilate says it is the Jews who are behind the accusation of Jesus. Jesus' answer, then, is double-edged: his followers will not fight against the Romans (who are behind Pilate's power) or against the Jews (his accusers).

With this answer Jesus eliminates two prevalent political options of his day: the armed defense of the Roman Empire, and the violent imposition of religious theocracy by the Jews. Neither Jesus nor his followers will fight violently to maintain the geographical boundaries of the Roman Empire or to further the religious defense of Judaism. The nationalist/imperialist and theocratic movements of this world cannot expect the support of Jesus' political movement.

This response resonates with the temptations of Jesus in the desert: to govern over all of the nations, or to ask for armies (hosts) of angels to rescue him from his dilemma (see Matt. 4:1–11). Neither imperialist power nor theocratic power are in the political option Jesus presents to his people. The politics of Jesus are not imposed by military power or by religious obligation. This is important for understanding Jesus' political option.

However, Jesus' response is not simply a no; it is also a yes. With his answer Jesus indicates he and his followers are willing to suffer and to die for the alternative values they propose for society. This proposal goes far beyond the immediate effectiveness of the movement. Jesus suggests that the commitment to life extends even to the point of giving one's own life so that others can live through this sacrifice. Life wins, with this proposal, and death loses. Life transcends all geographic criteria, all doctrine and religious dogma. Life is a value that does not originate in this world but in God.

Another aspect of this response is the communitarian element of Jesus' option. A community has decided not to fight for these things. It is a voluntary community, a community that acts like this because of its solidarity with the values of another kingdom. You could say the other kingdom is a community of values, a community that desires life for all, regardless of borders or race. Jesus actually offers a political option to save the world from self-destruction. Formation of the community committed to the new kingdom is the basic strategy: after being tempted to go in other directions, Jesus organizes his community; after becoming discouraged with Jesus' death, the disciples organize themselves into a community of the Spirit. The ministry of this new church is to offer this communitarian option to the world, founded upon Jesus' example and the power present in the Spirit. The option of his kingdom is the option of community.

It is important to note that this communitarian option is not simply to:
- strengthen and relax us so we can better practice our everyday jobs in the world;
- give ourselves over as necessary fodder so the world can continue on its path;
- fulfill the role of a sacred presence, which the world assigns to the church;
- care for sacred and mysterious treasures the world acknowledges as important;
- recharge our batteries so we can push the common values of the world even harder.

No. The formation of the community is a political option for the world. This community follows a different king and represents a true alternative: a kingdom that neither originates in nor moves toward worldly kingdoms. This is a real community, a nation of priests, a present kingdom, where:
- a certain level of equality exists between poor and rich, slave and free, women and men, children and parents;
- power rests on discerning and exercising each person's spiritual gifts;
- all strategies of imposition and hierarchy are left behind, and power is concentrated equally with all;

- violence is rejected as a strategy incompatible with its basic objectives;
- justice manifests itself, compassion is practiced, love is embodied, truth is heard and humility is seen;
- there is no theft, because each one has enough and does not envy another; there is no lying, because complete honesty is practiced; there is no violence, because transformation is voluntary; there is no bondage, because freedom is fundamental; there are no physical borders, because membership is not determined by race, geography, or ethnicity; there is no physical, emotional, or sexual abuse, because mutuality exists.

Does this seem like a real political option?❧

19

Christian victory:
Idealism or realism?

No irony is more pronounced in the New Testament than Jesus' words when facing the reality of the Cross:

> "In the world you face persecution. But take courage;
> I have conquered the world!" (John 16:33b)

Seems crazy, doesn't it? This humble carpenter from Nazareth, who is able to ally himself with some good-willed women and only twelve apostles, one of whom is a traitor and the other cowards; who attracts the opposition of religious and political powers against his tiny group; this carpenter on the eve of being betrayed, handed over, misunderstood, captured, tortured, condemned, abused, stripped, beaten and crucified, says, "I have conquered the world." And he did not say so craftly, thinking all of this was about to get better. No. He warns, "In the world you face persecution."

He seems to say that the coming of persecution is a victory, that to die is to be victorious.

How should we understand this unshakable faith? Is this inflated idealism? Is this putting one's head in the sand, like an ostrich? Is this an emotionally unbalanced hope?

We are here confronted with a basic question: How can the path that points to the cross and death be hopeful?

Many answers have been suggested:

- Some say that our sins are forgiven on the Cross and this is how the Cross gives us hope for eternal life after death, and that is the victory.

- Others say that Jesus bore all of the world's sins on his shoulders on the cross, and, by concentrating them in one place, tied to the death of one man, the power of sin in the world was broken, and this fact gives us hope.

- Others will say that the fact that Jesus walked the way of the cross means we are free from such a burden, and this, of course, is good news.

- Others say that with the Cross God paid the ransom, the price of liberation from the devil, and with this purchase we are liberated from Satan's bondage.

- Others prefer to look at the psychological importance of the Cross. The Cross reminds us of our own mortality. To overcome means to conquer the fear of death. Life is more wholesome when we recognize human mortality.

- Others see the Cross as a model, an example, a pedagogical tool to understand the reality of life. The Cross shows us the way.

- Others say that salvation and hope came to us not so much by way of the cross but by the spilling of blood, and the Cross fulfilled this requirement.

These varied responses show that the struggle to find hope in the event of the Cross has been continual and difficult. What motivates this search is, in part, our acknowledgment that the Cross was grotesque and repugnant.

Despite having beautified the cross in our modern world—using it as a decoration, jewelry, art and magic wand—in our hearts we recognize that the Cross was ugly, painful and cruel.

That is why Jesus' words, "I have conquered the world," seem so ironic to us, so difficult to understand.

The biblical text itself provides clues that help us understand the hope that exists in the Cross:

- The Bible speaks of the Cross as a fact in Christian life, not as a goal or an obligation. The Cross is to be neither sought nor avoided; it is to be neither adored nor cursed. It is a fact, a reality, a logical presence for those who seek to transform the world.

- The crucifixion, in first-century Jerusalem, was a particular event, but the Bible interprets it as having cosmic significance. The Cross was a historical event, but the Bible's authors explain it as a fact of universal significance.

Although the Cross was a human and historical event, the Bible also interprets it as an eschatological and ontological one. Because of this event, something radically and fundamentally changed in the universe. According to the New Testament, human history is divided into two parts: before and after the Cross.

The triumph of God on the cross was a triple judgment:

1. The world judged God, and the world clearly pronounced its preference over and against the divine will.
2. The world judged itself. The world's process of self-judgment in the face of the will of God was a victory for God. The world could no longer make any sacred pretenses.
3. On the cross God judged the world. The true intentions of human powers were unmasked in the face of the divine will. What many had suspected turned out to be true, and this revelation was a victory for God.

Fundamentally, these judgments had to do with the fact that the world saw the presence of God in Jesus as a heresy. Imagine! On the cross the world declared God to be heretical, and with this declaration tried to sacralize (divinize) the sinful structure of the world. If God were heretical, then human structures would be orthodox; that is, the world must be judged to be right and correct.

The judgment of God in the Cross rejects, denies and judges all cultures and religions that propose other gods who are not aligned with Jesus and proclaims them unworthy of our loyalty. The Cross contradicts their wisdom (1 Cor. 1:18) and crucifies their law and their world (Gal. 2:20; 6:14).

The Cross, then, provides the foundation for Christian spirituality. The Spirit of Christianity is the Spirit of Christ, Christ crucified.

The New Testament offers a post-Resurrection perspective; that is, they interpret the Cross from the perspective of the Resurrection. The triumph on the cross is confidently proclaimed after the

Resurrection experience. By the Resurrection, one knows true life in God grows from the path of the Cross.

The direct, intimate and inseparable relationship between the Cross and the Resurrection gives us the fundamental clue for finding hope in the Cross. Resurrection, not death, is the final word of God. God's yes in the Resurrection cancels the human no of the Cross. With the Resurrection we know that:

- the path chosen by Jesus was the right one;
- the obedience proposed by Jesus was the true one;
- the ethic discerned by Jesus was the will of his Father; and,
- the strategy proposed by Jesus was the correct one.

The Cross brings to light the criteria necessary to discern the path of salvation, liberation and reconciliation. These are the criteria of the Crucified One, and this revelation is a great victory.

This is why Jesus can say with confidence: "I have conquered the world," and, at the same time, "In the world you face persecution" (John 16:33).

The power of God revealed in human weakness is the secret of the victory on the cross. Paul says:

> I did not come proclaiming the mystery of God to you in lofty words or wisdom. For I decided to know nothing among you except Jesus Christ, and him crucified . . . so that your faith might not rest on human wisdom but on the power of God. (1 Cor. 2:1b-2, 5)

The political and religious regimes of Jesus' time did not understand this secret of the power of God.

> None of the rulers of this age understood this [wisdom]; for if they had, they would not have crucified the Lord of glory. (1 Cor. 2:8)

How interesting! According to this passage the crucifixion was the fruit of human ignorance, not the will of God. If they had recognized the will of God in Jesus, the powers would not have crucified Jesus; they would have given themselves over to God's will.

Truly, the Cross continues to be the single historical event that functions as the seed of the world's salvation. In this truth lies the

Christian hope. It is this truth that provides a foundation for our spirituality and our mission as disciples of the Crucified One.

It is important to note that Christian hope is neither pure idealism nor mere realism; it is both. Christian hope is based in the reality of the Cross, an ugly death that resulted in life. This truth, confidently projected toward the future, is the Christian's real and ideal hope. There is no reason to doubt:

- that God's will for our future is no different than it was for Jesus. God's will continues to be the path of the Cross;
- that God's will for us is that the same power of life, manifested in the resurrection of the Crucified One, will continue to manifest itself in our lives and in our world;
- that human ignorance in the face of the divine will continues to be today's spiritual battle; and,
- that the same power of the resurrection made known in Jesus continues to reveal itself in the life of the humanly weak who are able to discern and put into practice the will of God in our world.

Christian victory is rooted in this confident hope, based on the Cross of Jesus.

Part 5

20

The spirituality
of spiritual disciplines

Having read this far, you may say: This book is really strange. I have not found what I expected to find in a book about spirituality. Yet, what I didn't expect, that I did find. This book speaks of sex, money, power, violence, politics, structures and community, but it does not mention conventional spiritual disciplines such as fasting, prayer, speaking in tongues, meditation, praise and healing. Maybe the author was mistaken when he selected the subtitle for the book?

No, I was not mistaken. I cannot speak of Christian spirituality and mission without speaking about the Christian life, the Christian task and the Christian goal. All spirituality is embodied in concrete ways or expressions of life. And I do want to comment on the importance of what are called spiritual disciplines.

However, since the previously mentioned spiritual disciplines raise numerous suspicions, accusations and/or doctrinal justifications in the Latin American context, I will begin by focusing on three biblical examples that may seem somewhat irrelevant and removed from our own reality. This will allow for what I like to call objective distance. If we can understand something that seems somewhat removed, I believe it will be easier to apply lessons learned to the disciplines that touch us more closely.

Let's reflect upon spiritual disciplines by looking briefly at biblical teaching regarding these three: (1) the tabernacle, (2) the Sabbath, and (3) circumcision.

The tabernacle: The sanctification of space

For the Hebrew people, the tabernacle represented the meeting place
where the holiness and glory of God were present:

> It shall be a regular burnt offering throughout your
> generations at the entrance of the tent of meeting
> before the LORD, where I will meet with you, to speak
> to you there. I will meet with the Israelites there, and
> it shall be sanctified by my glory; I will consecrate the
> tent of meeting and the altar. . . . I will dwell among
> the Israelites, and I will be their God. And they shall
> know that I am the LORD their God, who brought them
> forth out of the land of Egypt that I might dwell among
> them; I am the LORD their God. (Exod. 29:42–46)

The tabernacle represented the mobile presence of God in the
midst of God's pilgrim people. The tabernacle was not the temple;
the tabernacle was not identified with one place, one land, one nation, one city or one mountain (see Exod. 25, 26; Ezek. 1–3). The
tabernacle was the symbol of a God of the road, a symbol useful for
a pilgrim people. It was the guarantee of God's presence in all places,
useful for a people who would become present in all places.

The tabernacle sanctified all space. The tabernacle reaffirmed
what Genesis had already taught: that all of creation, all of the world,
is the milieu for the action, presence and holiness of the Creator
God (Gen. 1—2).

The tabernacle was also a reminder of what God had done in
the Exodus, liberating the people from slavery: "They shall know
that I am the LORD their God, who brought them forth out of the
land of Egypt" (Exod. 29:45). The people recognized God as a lib-
erator God, a God who acted to liberate God's people from oppression, slavery and unjust conditions in Egypt. The tabernacle is a
reminder, a "regular burnt offering," of the will of God in the Exodus.
This is why Jews still celebrate the Feast of Tabernacles and the Pass-
over, remembering the liberation promoted by God in the Exodus.

The tabernacle not only sanctifies space, it also sanctifies the liberating action of God in space. The tabernacle permanently proclaims that this liberating will of God is no accident; it represents the permanent will of God, in all places, for all people.

The discipline of permanently encountering God in God's meeting place is an important discipline for the people of God. Biblical teaching about the tabernacle sanctifies all such meeting places and desacralizes all space where this encounter does not exist. This teaching has important implications for how we exercise spiritual disciplines.

The Sabbath: The sanctification of time

Parallel to the sanctification of space by the presence of the tabernacle, we find the sanctification of time through the spiritual discipline of the Sabbath. As the tabernacle signified a sanctuary of the divine presence within the space of a pilgrim people, so the Sabbath represented a sanctuary of time within the everyday tasks of the people.

> Remember the sabbath day, and keep it holy. . . .
> Therefore the LORD blessed the sabbath day and consecrated it. (Exod. 20:8, 11b)

Just as the tabernacle was a celebration of God's liberating power in the Exodus, the Sabbath celebrates God's creative power in creation:

> And on the seventh day God finished the work that he had done, and he rested on the seventh day from all the work that he had done. So God blessed the seventh day and hallowed it, because on it God rested from all the work that he had done in creation. (Gen. 2:2–3)

This is the first biblical reference to "hallowing" (sanctification) or "holiness." The Sabbath is the first of what is sanctified in the Bible; that is, time is sanctified before space is. We can fight for land, discuss doctrine, debate about forms of worship or praise a beautiful church building, but the first connection to God is through time. Time is sacred and sanctified (hallowed).

It is also important to note that the seventh day is not isolated from the others. The rest of God on the seventh day is intimately linked to the fact that the work of the other six days "was very good" (Gen. 1:31). The other six days sanctify the seventh, and the seventh day blesses the effort exerted during the previous six. If the works done on the six days are not "good," we should not try to "sanctify" them with a Sabbath. The Sabbath celebration is based on the success of the other six days. The existence of the Sabbath is designed to sanctify all of our time as God's gift to us, and it symbolizes our obedience to God.

The Sabbath is not a legality aimed at making life difficult for us. It is a celebration of God's faithfulness to God's people. The Sabbath is a gift to help us enjoy what God gives us; it is to help us redouble our efforts to follow the steps of obedience to God. The Sabbath represents the joy that expresses our confidence in God the provider. In modern Judaism, the liturgy to celebrate the coming of the Sabbath is like a wedding celebration. Erotic passages from the Song of Solomon are the text; a chorus to welcome the bride is sung. This marriage celebration joyfully unites the people with the bride, the Sabbath, to again re-create themselves according to the will of God.

Just as the tabernacle blesses and sanctifies the space of the action of God's people, the Sabbath blesses and sanctifies the time of this effort. To sanctify time and space is like saying: The vocation of this people is sacred; the God of this vocation is holy. Hallowed (sanctified) be the God who sanctifies the space and time of God's people.

It should not surprise us that the Bible unites these two disciplines:

> You shall keep my sabbaths and reverence my sanctuary: I am the LORD. (Lev. 19:30)

Circumcision: The sanctification of the covenant between God and God's people
The covenant God made with God's people will be perpetually visible to all those who have contact with this people in space and time. This visible sign will be the circumcision of males on the eighth day:

> This is my covenant, which you shall keep, between
> me and you and your offspring after you: Every male
> among you shall be circumcised. . . . and it shall be a
> sign of the covenant between me and you. Through-
> out your generations every male among you shall be
> circumcised when he is eight days old. . . . So shall
> my covenant be in your flesh an everlasting covenant.
> (Gen. 17:10–13)

The first question that arises is: Why circumcision on the eighth day? Why not on the tenth, seventh, first or fourth day? The answer takes into account two issues: (1) Circumcisions needs to be performed as soon as possible after birth; and (2) observing the Sabbath (the consecration of time) has priority in the child's life.

The eighth day is the first day that guarantees that both prerequisites are fulfilled. The eighth day guarantees that the child has already observed one Sabbath, and at the same time, that the circumcision is done as soon as possible after birth. Just as the sanctification of time precedes the sanctification of space, so too the Creator emphasizes his relationship with the newborn through consecrated time (the Sabbath) before doing so through the sign of the covenant (circumcision). Circumcision is the symbol of the covenant with God within the time of God; it symbolizes the people's identity within God's consecrated time; it demonstrates the people's vocational calling within the space and time God gives to them.

It's not a coincidence that this identification as God's people occurs on the male sexual organ. Circumcision is not simply performed for health reasons, as some suggest. The penis transmits the identity and perpetuity of the people. To make the penis different is to magnify the consecration (separateness) that distinguishes the people. In a previous chapter we spoke of sex as a public act. Circumcision supports this perspective. The people's life is defined by its identity with the covenant with God.

Circumcision is also a spiritual discipline. As Christians we prefer to apply Jeremiah's teaching that true circumcision is of the heart. But the purpose of circumcision, even that of the heart, has not changed. The spiritual discipline of God's people is a reflection of the integral nature of life, a sign of the sanctification of the entire vocation of the people.

Circumcision dramatizes the fact that the kingdom of the people of God is a political option for the world. To identify with this kingdom means to hand over all of one's identity and vocation to this kingdom.

We have investigated three spiritual disciplines we find in the Bible, disciplines that we may not pay much attention to in Christian doctrine and practice. These have to do with the consecration of space, time and the identity and vocation of the people.

Can we make the necessary connections to apply these disciplines to spiritual disciplines of our time? Do these disciplines help us to understand the importance of spiritual disciplines? Why not do a little exercise? Take the usual disciplines, such as prayer, fasting and communion, and put them in the place of the three outlined here, while keeping the same explanations. You will find great spiritual enrichment. I guarantee it!

21

The spirit of worship, the worship of the Spirit

❧

Sometimes one hears the argument that Christian spirituality manifests itself most clearly in moments of worship, whether in the praise and adoration of evangelical worship or in the Roman Catholic worship of celebrating the Mass and administering the sacraments. Sometimes this argument is clinched with the statement that the Christian mission is to offer worship to God. This is a closed circuit—the mission is to offer worship, and by this offering we become spiritual.

With our theme of spirituality and mission, we must look more closely at the biblical teaching about worshiping God. We will do this by looking at some key texts.

Paul says:

> I appeal to you therefore, brothers and sisters, by the mercies of God, to present your bodies as a living sacrifice, holy and acceptable to God, which is your spiritual worship. Do not be conformed to this world, but be transformed by the renewing of your minds, so that you may discern what is the will of God— what is good and acceptable and perfect. (Rom. 12:1–2)

Let's look at this text, beginning from the end. The goal, Paul says, is to discern, validate or test the will of God. This subject sounds familiar. We spoke previously of the important task of discerning spirits. Here we have the same emphasis. This proof will not be easy; it requires the renewing of our mind (understanding).

This transformation changes us enough to prove the good will of God and allows us not to conform ourselves "to this world," an interesting phrase, since it presupposes that the direction of this world does not reflect the will of God. Not conforming ourselves to this world, Paul says, entails a "sacrifice"; that is, the life of nonconformity will be difficult, sacrificial and misunderstood by those of the world. Nonetheless, it is precisely this "living sacrifice" that we present to God as our worship. But ours is not just any worship; it is a "spiritual worship, which we could translate literally as the logical service that we offer to the world.

Note the chain that ends in worship:
- discernment of the will of God for the world;
- transformation of our mind, our way of seeing things;
- renewal of the mind transforms us, we are no longer as we were before. This means that we do not conform ourselves to the direction of the world;
- this transformation implies a tension, a living sacrifice;
- this sacrifice is our logical service, which is called worship.

In a few words, the best worship we can offer to God is to live transformed lives over against the demands of the world. True worship is the nonconformist relationship with the world that is a real service to the world; worship is a favor that we offer to the world. It makes sense. By doing this favor we offer the world an alternative, an option. People search for alternatives, and here is one.

Paul shows us some implications of this service, this worship we offer. Chapters 12 to 15 of Romans give us many precise clues for how to live in nonconformity to the world as our service to God. Let's look at some of these. We each are to:
- measure one's own ability (12:3);
- take everyone's gifts into account, not only our own (12:6);
- behave as a body, not individuals (12:4–8);
- not be lazy but diligent (12:11);
- rejoice in hope (12:12);
- be patient in tribulation (12:12);
- be constant in prayer (12:12);
- share with the poor (12:13);
- practice hospitality (12:13);

- bless and not curse those who persecute us (12:14);
- rejoice with those who rejoice (12:15);
- weep with those who weep (12:15);
- be humble (12:16);
- not repay evil with evil (12:17);
- live peaceably with all, if possible (12:18);
- not avenge ourselves (12:19);
- give food and drink to our enemy (12:20);
- overcome evil with good (12:21);
- discern the work of the governing authorities (13:1–7);
- love everyone (vv. 8–14); and,
- care for our relations with the weak (14:1–23).

Looking at each of these suggestions, we can appreciate why Romans claims to be nonconformist: the world does not operate according to these rules. Indeed, the world often

- does not share with the needy;
- kills the enemy;
- imposes itself;
- is proud;
- takes revenge; and,
- takes food away from the enemy.

It really is a service or worship to offer an alternative such as this to the world, which needs it.

According to the prophet Amos, God says:

> I hate, I despise your festivals,
>   and I take no delight in your solemn assemblies.
> Even though you offer me your burnt offerings and
>   grain offerings,
>   I will not accept them;
> and the offerings of well-being of your fatted animals
>   I will not look upon.
> Take away from me the noise of your songs;
>   I will not listen to the melody of your harps.
> But let justice roll down like waters,
>   and righteousness like an ever-flowing stream.
>   (Amos 5:21–24)

According to this passage, God becomes tired of the offerings, songs, instruments and religious festivals of God's people. People worship God, bringing vegetables and fatted animals as peace offerings. They come with their songs and instruments and try to celebrate and to worship God. But Amos says God hates and despises this worship. Why? The last line gives us the reason: there is no justice, there is no righteousness.

If righteousness and justice are not found among God's people, then attempts at worship contradict the foundation of their existence. God is just, and if people want to worship God, they need to be practicing justice as well. If they do not, then the character of the praise goes against the character of the One being praised. There is no congruence and hence no acceptable worship.

This teaching regarding worship acceptable to God reminds us of the words of Micah. He too asks how we should present ourselves before God, if we should worship with offerings, calves, rams, oil, and our firstborn. His answer is similar to Amos's:

> He has told you, O mortal, what is good;
>   and what does the LORD require of you
> but to do justice, and to love kindness,
>   and to walk humbly with your God? (Mic. 6:8)

The message of the prophets is clear: there is a prerequisite for appropriate worship. It is the presence of congruence. Is the one who praises aligned with the One being praised? Is there congruence between the one who offers and the One who receives worship? If this prerequisite is not fulfilled, then all attempts at worship fail. Either worship is a celebrative fruit of obedience, or it is nothing.

Isaiah also touches on the topic of worship acceptable to God, this time focusing on fasting. According to the prophet, the people ask God the following questions:

> "Why do we fast, but you do not see?
>   Why humble ourselves, but you do not notice?" (Isa. 58:3)

But God has told them the answer:

> Yet day after day they seek me,
>   and delight to know my ways,

as if they were a nation that practiced righteousness
and did not forsake the ordinance of their God;
they ask of me righteous judgments,
they delight to draw near to God. (Isa. 58:2)

The prophet then outlines what God considers to be an acceptable fast, a metaphorical fast with the following characteristics (Isa. 58:3–14):

- it does not exploit workers;
- it loosens the bonds of wickedness;
- it undoes the thongs of the yoke;
- it lets the oppressed go free;
- it breaks every yoke;
- it shares bread with the hungry;
- it brings the homeless poor into one's house; and
- it covers the neighbor who is naked.

Then your light shall break forth like the dawn,
and your healing shall spring up quickly;
your vindicator shall go before you,
the glory of the Lord shall be your rear guard.
Then you shall call, and the Lord will answer;
you shall cry for help, and he will say, Here I am.
(Isa. 58:8–9)

These teachings from Paul, Amos, Micah and Isaiah remind us of Jesus' own teaching:

So when you are offering your gift at the altar, if you remember that your brother or sister has something against you, leave your gift there before the altar and go; first be reconciled to your brother or sister, and then come and offer your gift. (Matt. 5:23–24)

Worship acceptable to God has to do with one's life before and parallel to the act of worship. Acceptable liturgy is not new praise. It is rather like a mirror; it is a reflection of prior praise manifested in the obedient life of the participant. God does not desire the sacrament of rigid routine, or the act itself, but the obedience that overflows into song, faithfulness that bolsters itself with prayer and fasting.

It is not that our mission is simply to praise, but that by being engaged in mission we experience so much of God's love, mercy, strength and protection that we cannot help but thank the God of mission. It is not that praise demonstrates our spirituality, but that our spirituality is communicated by praise. The sequence is important: worship is the fruit of integral life, not a guarantee of this integral life.❧

22

The spirit of prayer, the prayer of the Spirit

It is likely that no discipline is considered more spiritual, no answer more automatic, no reflection more genuine, no echo more natural in the popular spirituality of Latin America than the spontaneous prayer of its people.

Phrases such as *si Dios quiere* (if God wills), *Dios mio* (my God), *O Jesús* (O Jesus), *si la virgin no meta la pata* (if the Virgin doesn't interfere), *virgin Maria* (Virgin Mary), *que Dios le bendiga* (may God bless you) and *padre nuestro* (our Father) are only a few of those we hear daily in the buses, streets, churches, places of employment and in the everyday conversations of the people. These words echo the longer prayers and more formal petitions we find in the liturgies of our worship services and Masses.

Our popular religiosity expresses itself in prayer. Let's reflect more deeply on some characteristics of prayer as an exercise of Christian spirituality.

A response
The initiative comes from God. Prayer is a human response to the divine initiative. As such, it is not necessary for prayer to be perfect, pure or well articulated. A groaning of the soul in the face of the

divine initiative is prayer as well. The psalmist describes prayer as a response:

> "Come," my heart says, "seek his face!"
> Your face, Lord, do I seek." (Ps. 27:8)

As a response, human prayer recognizes God's initiative as an act of grace. Grace is *gratis*. It is free; it is voluntary. God's initiative is not deserved and cannot be bought. Prayer cannot be the human manipulation of God. Prayer does not force the hand of God in our favor. Prayer is not magic.

Attention to God

Human prayer is to pay attention to God, to concentrate our mind on a possible word of God for us. The mind that prays is alert and open. God answers in many ways. The mind that expects God's answer in only one place, one time or one form can easily miss God's word and presence.

A search

Prayer is the serious search for the *will* of God. God is present before, during and after prayer. It is not necessary to search for God. Prayer attempts to plug into God's permanent presence in order to understand God's will in our lives. The permanent presence of God means that prayer is not meant to add or mold God to our life. Rather, prayer means to suspend enough of our concerns to allow contact with God's presence. To speak in a mathematical sense, prayer is not a process of addition but one of subtraction; prayer does not add something that was not there but removes obstacles that separate us from recognizing God's presence.

An instrument of reconciliation

Prayer is an instrument of human reconciliation. It is very difficult to hate someone if we pray for him or her. It is very difficult to kill someone for whom we have prayed. Prayer places the other as a valuable person in the eyes of God. As such, it is difficult to denigrate those we pray for, and reconciliation with that person becomes easier. Prayer is not a substitute for human effort, but the companion to the supplicant's work. Jesus tells us a parable of a tiresome widow who kept demanding that the judge "grant [her] justice against [her] opponent" (Luke 18:3). Finally, the judge gave in to her continual petitioning so she would leave him in peace. The moral of the story is that we "need to pray always and not to lose heart" (Luke 18:1). Prayer does not replace prophetic activity but underscores it. Prayer is not an alternative to action but the alternative to inaction. Prayer accompanies effort, and prayer allows us to keep up our courage, to persist and to continue in the ministries of the Christian path.

Trust

Prayer denies human self-sufficiency. To pray means to search for wisdom somewhere else. To pray means to say, "I do not have the answer; I need help." Prayer is an act of trust in God's authority. To pray is to hand oneself over to a perspective that is not necessarily our own. Even Jesus says, "Not my will, but thine be done." It is not easy to submit our judgment to another's wisdom.

Prayer is not meant to justify what we are already doing. It's interesting how many times we hear that, through prayer, God confirms—the purchase of the car already in our garage, the presence of the man or woman in our life when we are already in bed together, or the new job we've already received the wage for. Sometimes it is difficult to distinguish between God's answer to our prayer and our own justification for our actions.

Community

Prayer does not replace the role of the community, but prayer underscores it. Many times the Christian community helps us to discern God's answer to our prayers.

Hope

Prayer confesses hope. Even desperate prayer presupposes hope, not only in our own abilities but in the power and promise of God. To say "Thy kingdom come" is the same as saying there is hope. First, we implore God to pay attention to our particular situation. Second, in asking this we begin to think about our responsibility regarding the situation at hand. Third, and perhaps most crucial, not only do we ask God to work in the situation and think of what we could do, we also ask God for the path we could follow under divine direction, aligned with God's will in the situation. Mature prayer travels along all three of these lanes simultaneously.

Gratitude

The prayer of gratitude to God is political prayer. Through prayer we thank God for our daily bread. We acknowledge that the business enterprise providing us the wage with which we buy bread is under God's rule.

We also thank God for protection during the night. Vigilante patrols and military and police forces do not have the definitive power to guarantee protection. Only God does.

When we thank God for life and health, we place medical professionals in a position of dependence under the healing power of God.

And when we thank God for our country, we imply that ultimately it is not the military, armies or weapons that determine a nation's geographic borders. Borders are not sacred. God is the Lord of the nations as well.

What about prayers that are not answered? The Book of Revelation gives readers an interesting perspective on the unanswered prayers of the saints. Why does God not seem to answer the clamor for justice on the earth? The book says the elders in heaven hold bowls full of the prayers of the saints (Rev. 5:8) and cry in a loud voice for justice in the world, saying:

> "Sovereign Lord, holy and true, how long will it be before you judge and avenge our blood on the inhabitants of the earth?" (Rev. 6:10b)

This is the key question, one we also hear in our own context. How long? Why not now? The answer is:

> The rest of humankind, who were not killed by these plagues, did not repent. . . . And they did not repent of their murders or their sorceries or their fornication or their thefts. (Rev. 9:20–21)

> People gnawed their tongues in agony, and . . . did not repent of their deeds. (Rev. 16:10c, 11c)

According to these passages, the explanation for the delay in answering the saints' prayers is none other than the compassion, mercy, patience and perseverance of God. This is really nothing new. God wants everyone to have enough time to repent. God does not want to take this opportunity away from anyone. If remembered, this perspective will help us in our life of prayer. God does not want revenge; God wants salvation for everyone.

According to this teaching from Revelation, prayer, important as it may be, must also align itself with God's priorities. As always, the first priority is abundant life for everyone. God makes room for compassion, mercy, forgiveness and repentance. Prayer does not replace this ministry of life but accompanies it.

Prayer is not the hammer of the weak; it is not the escape of the fearful; it is not the refuge of the irresponsible; it is not hiding one's head like an ostrich. Prayer is the personal and community instrument of communion in the Spirit of God.

Christian prayer, then, is the expression of spirituality and as such is the foundation to ensure that the mission is of God and not simply of ourselves.

23

Vice and virtue: The flesh and the Spirit

There is a story about two farmers. One wants to buy the other's mule. The owner exaggerates the mule's qualities: strong, young, obedient, hardworking and always responsive to the owner's commands. The other farmer is interested in seeing the mule and how it handles the plow. They go to the farm, and the owner gets ready. Before beginning, however, the owner takes a large stick and smacks the mule on the head.

"Wait a minute," the buyer says. "You told me it always responds and obeys. Why did you hit it?"

The owner answers: "Of course it obeys, but I have to get its attention first."

It seems to me that this is how the apostle Paul addresses this topic with his readers. What does it mean to live in the Spirit? Paul approaches the subject with two big sticks: one is the stick of what living in the Spirit does *not* mean, that is, his list of vices; and the second is the stick of what this life *does* mean, that is, his list of the fruit of the Spirit.

Paul does not just name a few ideas. He uses forty-two different words to refer to thirty-nine vices and twenty words to refer to the sixteen virtues that emerge as fruit of the Spirit. We won't investigate all of these concepts here, but we can outline the general direction of his teaching (see 1 Cor. 5:9–11; 6:9–10; 13; 2 Cor. 6:3–10; 12:20–21; Rom. 1:29–31; Gal. 5:19–21; 5:22–23; 1 Thess. 5:12–25). We will concentrate here on Galatians 5.

The walk

Paul places the issue of vices and virtues within a broad perspective: the Christian walk.

> But I say, walk by the Spirit. (Gal. 5:16a, RSV)

> If we live by the Spirit, let us also walk by the Spirit. (Gal. 5:25, RSV)

Although the word *walk* is used in both cases in the English translation, the Greek uses two different words. Verse 16 uses *peripateo*, which literally refers to the routine of walking: what we do to move from one place to another. This routine is now accomplished "in the Spirit"; that is, our walking has direction and a destination. In verse 25, the word is *stoicheo*, which means a fixed direction, a trip along a predetermined route or norm. Now this route is defined by "the Spirit." Vices and virtues are not defined primarily as particular acts but as directions, routes, orientations that may or may not reflect the presence of the Spirit in the walk.

Freedom

Galatians 5 also gives us clues as to the direction of this path. It is the path toward freedom:

> For freedom Christ has set us free. Stand firm, therefore, and do not submit again to a yoke of slavery. (5:1)

> For you were called to freedom. (5:13a)

Paul makes special reference to two enemies of freedom, two things that run against the freedom of the Spirit: the law (5:1–12) and the flesh (5:13–26). I suspect these two may even be synonymous for him. The law is the mutilation of the flesh, symbolized by circumcision; and the flesh is the mutilation of the law, symbolized by vices (5:19–21). On the other hand, the law of the Spirit is the law of Christ:

"You shall love your neighbor as yourself." (5:14b)

Therefore, to live in freedom is not to live without law; rather, it is a change of law. Freedom means to live under the law of Christ (Gal. 6:2), rejecting "freedom as an opportunity for self-indulgence" (5:13). The freedom of the Spirit has the parameters of Jesus.

The vices
The first thing to note when looking at the list of vices is that the majority are social vices; that is, vices that break and tear apart the life of the community of the Spirit. They are vices such as enmity, strife, jealousy, anger, selfishness, dissension, carousing and envy (5:20–21). Clearly these are values that destroy the importance of community life. Vices are those things that mar the fundamental work of the Spirit, which is the formation of a community of the Spirit. Even the vices we often classify as personal, such as fornication, drunkenness and carousing (5:19–21), are bad because of their effect upon the community. There is no sin that is purely personal. Vices, like the rejection of the desires of the Spirit in our lives, are a rejection of the Christian community. And they are serious faults. Vices violate both the purity and direction of the community and end up distorting the truth of its message.

Note that Paul does not become discouraged with the human condition. Paul does not make up items to include on these lists. These vices are actual problems and conditions present in the churches to which he writes. Drunkenness, fornication, envy, dissension, orgies and more occurred in the churches of Galatia, Corinth, Thessalonica and Rome. These were not Paul's inventions. Yet he continues to say that even these troubled churches are the church of Christ. Paul had unquenchable faith in the possibility of transformation under the power of the Spirit. He was hopeful.

Virtues
The virtues of the Spirit are expressed in one word: *fruit* (singular, as in Gal. 5:22). One might ask, why does Paul speak of "works" (5:19) when talking about the flesh, and "fruit" (5:22) when talking

about the Spirit? Why not speak about the works of the Spirit? I think there are good reasons for carefully choosing these words:

- to emphasize that the fruit is a gift of the Spirit and not a result of human effort;
- to emphasize that these virtues are qualities of the Spirit within us; and,
- to emphasize that although many works can destroy the community, only one fruit can unite it: the presence of the Spirit directing the efforts of the community.

Once again we note that the virtues are mostly social qualities, characteristics that edify and maintain the community. They are "love, joy, peace, patience, kindness, generosity, faithfulness, gentleness, and self-control" (5:22–23a). The purpose of these virtues is so there will be no "competing against one another, envying one another" (5:26). These are essential communitarian goals.

It is important to distinguish between the fruit of the Spirit and the outcome of human strategy. I know someone who was a Christian missionary in a Muslim country for twenty-eight years without having one convert to Christianity. We could say this was not much of a result, but we cannot say he did not show the fruit of the Spirit. He was widely recognized for his life of love, his acts of justice, his patience, kindness, gentleness, and his goodness with people. But for various reasons, death threats included, people did not openly give themselves over to the Lord Jesus.

In the evangelical world we sometimes hear that "many were converted as fruit of the campaign." With our emphasis on relevance, effectiveness and results, we sometimes think each success is fruit and each failure is a lack of fruit. I do not believe this is what Paul teaches. Goodness is fruit of the Spirit even when it is taken advantage of. Patience is fruit despite resulting in failure. The love of an enemy is fruit even if the enemy responds by killing us. This focus acquires even more meaning when we remember that Paul speaks of fruit as the communitarian manifestation of the Spirit. A community of peace—one that lives in peace, that teaches peace, that struggles for peace, that demonstrates peace—is fruit of the Spirit even when society rejects this community and does not accept its teaching. The nonviolence of Jesus was fruit of the Spirit even though it resulted in the violence of the Cross.

In faith we can say that the fruit of the Spirit will produce genuine results. Through the confidence of faith, we can also admit that, in some cases, the presence of the fruit of the Spirit has not yet had measurable success. Fruit of the Spirit such as faith, joy and hope nurtures us even when results are not visible. Someone has said that Christian hope is not optimism; hope is what we have left when it is impossible to be optimistic. I believe this saying expresses the difference between fruit and results very well.

Application
- the Spirit desires freedom
- freedom in the Spirit is the destination of the walk
- freedom in the Spirit is the path toward the destination
- freedom in the Spirit is the end and the means simultaneously
- freedom is found by subjecting oneself to the law of Christ
- the law of Christ is a communitarian law
- to subject oneself to Christ is to subject oneself to Christ's community
- the path toward freedom is a communitarian path
- the communitarian path leads to freedom of the Spirit
- the vice of the flesh is to deny the community as foundational
- the fruit of the Spirit is to build upon and trust this foundation
- that which is fruit for the Spirit is a gift for the Christian
- the Christian community receives this gift
- that which is fruit for the Spirit is seed for the Christian
- the Christian community sows this fruit of the Spirit
- the harvest of this sown fruit is the opening for the action of the Spirit
- the bigger the opening, the more fruit will be sown

> Finally, beloved, whatever is true, whatever is honorable, whatever is just, whatever is pure, whatever is pleasing, whatever is commendable, if there is any excellence and if there is anything worthy of praise, think about these things. Keep on doing the things you have learned and received and heard and seen in me, and the God of peace will be with you. (Phil. 4:8–9)

24

The spirit of forgiveness, the forgiveness of the Spirit

How to deal with sin? How to conquer evil? How to counteract the Fall? These are key questions for the mission of God.

If we consider God to be the first missionary to the world, what would be God's objectives? God's goals? Scripture suggests that the principal objective of the mission of God toward the world is to deal with sin so as to re-create the world according to God's original intent.

As John the Elder bluntly declares:

> The Son of God was revealed for this purpose, to destroy the works of the devil. (1 John 3:8b)

The apostle Paul confirms this:

> God chose . . . things that are not, to reduce to nothing things that are. (1 Cor. 1:28)

> God . . . calls into existence the things that do not exist. (Rom. 4:17)

But it is not just the task of God and Jesus to "destroy the works of the devil"; this is what the church is for as well. The word *church* is mentioned in only two passages in the four gospels. And in both cases Jesus charges the church with the task of dealing with sin (see Matt. 16:17–19; 18:15–22).

We see the same emphasis in the Great Commission of the fourth Gospel. Jesus says:

> "Receive the Holy Spirit. If you forgive the sins of
> any, they are forgiven them; if you retain the sins of
> any, they are retained." (John 20:22c-23)

The church is charged with continuing the mission of the missionary God: to deal with sin, in order to re-create the world, so as to counteract the Fall.

But it is one thing to identify the task of mission and another to identify the strategy for this task. When we search in the biblical story for the strategy of mission, time after time we are confronted with stories of forgiveness. Forgiveness is one of the basic components of the strategy of God's mission in dealing with the sin of the world.

Jesus exemplifies this important component for dealing with evil:

> Then Jesus said, "Father, forgive them; for they do
> not know what they are doing." (Luke 23:34a)

Forgiveness is also the principal process with which the church has been entrusted.

> Then Peter came and said to him, "Lord, if another
> member of the church sins against me, how often
> should I forgive? As many as seven times?" Jesus said
> to him, "Not seven times, but, I tell you, seventy-seven
> times." (Matt. 18:21-22)

The Lord's Prayer (Matt. 6:9–15) teaches us to forgive and the parable of the unforgiving servant denounces the person who has received forgiveness but does not forgive (Matt. 18:23–35). The New Testament overflows with the primacy of forgiveness in Christian spirituality. First, God forgives, and so we too should forgive.

The New Testament constructs a chain of forgiveness in dealing with sin in the world and in the efforts to restore and reconcile the creation to its Creator.

But it is one thing to identify the task of mission as dealing with sin and another to identify forgiveness as the strategy with which to accomplish this task. And it is still another to understand the essence of the forgiveness that God gives us and asks of us. We now turn to reflect further on this understanding.

First, it is important to point out that addressing the issue of forgiveness is not easy for us in today's world. I remember being in Montevideo, Uruguay, as the country was discussing what to do with the previous military juntas and dictators who had ruled prior to the current civilian and democratic government. These dictators had committed grave injustices against humanity. Some proposed punishment, others desired forgiveness, still others proposed an impartial judicial process that would decide their fate in a mature and democratic manner. The same discussion has occurred in Chile, Argentina, Brazil, Paraguay and El Salvador. In North America the issue of forgiveness currently enters debates regarding cases of sexual abuse, incestuous relations and the physical abuse of children and spouses. This problem is also discussed in relation to capital punishment, which took the lives of fifty-six offenders in the United States in 1995 alone, with more than fourteen hundred people currently on death row waiting their turn.

Questions arise about the relationship between forgiveness and justice, between mercy and justice, between forgiveness and repentance, as well as about just payment for sins committed, the healing and recuperation of victims, and the institutionalization of cultural and political improvements to guarantee a better future.

It is worthwhile, then, to investigate more closely biblical teachings regarding the role of forgiveness in Christian spirituality and in dealing with sin.

The New Testament uses the words *forgiveness (afesis)* and *forgive (afiemi)* 163 times. They are commonly used words in the Greek language and contain a richness of meaning that is important to understand:

- freedom, liberation, to let go; for example, in Jesus' announcement in the synagogue in Nazareth, he points out

that to receive the Spirit of God means "to proclaim release
[afesis] to the captives" and "to set at liberty [afesis] those
who are oppressed" (Luke 4:18, RSV);

- to yield up, to emit, to utter; for example, Jesus "yielded up
  [afiemi] his spirit" (Matt. 27:50, RSV), "uttered [afiemi] a loud
  cry" (Mark 15:37, RSV);
- to leave, to concede, to allow; for example, Jesus says, "Let
  them alone [afiemi]; they are blind guides of the blind" (Matt.
  15:14);
- to neglect; for example, Jesus says, "You . . . have neglected
  [afiemi] the weightier matters of the law" (Matt. 23:23);
- to leave behind; for example, the author of Hebrews says,
  "Therefore let us go on, . . . leaving behind [afiemi] the basic
  teaching about Christ" (Heb. 6:1);
- to leave; for example, "Then the fever left [afiemi] her" (Mark
  1:31);
- to resign, to concede, to surrender; for example, Jesus says,
  "Let [afiemi] him have your cloak as well" [Matt. 5:40, RSV];
- to relax, to forgive, to remit; for example, Jesus says that his
  blood is "poured out for many for the forgiveness [afesis] of
  sins" (Matt. 26:28).

I suspect that the manner in which forgiveness deals with sin
incorporates something of each of the meanings we have identified.
Let's look at some characteristics of "forgiveness" we can identify.

- Often forgiveness is for the benefit of others. It is to liberate
  them, allow them, leave them and give them a new start. It is
  characterized by mercy and grace.
- There are cases where forgiveness is an action of the powerful/
  innocent toward the weak/guilty, where the one who has the
  power to change the situation of the guilty does so because
  the weak cannot act for their own well-being. In this case
  forgiveness means to extend a hand to one who does not
  deserve it, for his or her benefit. It means to use one's influence,
  authority and power for the well-being and liberation of the
  weak or guilty.
- The fundamental role of the guilty party in the offer of
  forgiveness is repentance, which means a change of life.
- There are cases when the innocent victim extends forgiveness
  to the powerful/guilty, to the oppressor. The victim takes the
  initiative to "allow" or "concede" something that the oppressor
  had not even asked for or expected. Another example where

the victim takes the initiative to extend forgiveness to the oppressor is when, on the cross, Jesus says: "Father, forgive them; for they do not know what they are doing" (Luke 23:34). In this case the victim shows surprising initiative by asking God to forgive even the enemy.

To forgive is thus to ask for God's blessing, Jesus' own liberation and that of the oppressor, recognizing that the victim might not be in a position to significantly change the situation of the sinner. In these cases the innocent one opens a door. To take advantage of this opening, the guilty/powerful parties need to repent and change their way of life. If the oppressor does not change, the offer remains, the door stays open, but the path of justice and reconciliation is untraveled.

- There are cases where both the powerful and weak parties consider each other innocent; the guilty party is beyond them both. In these cases solidarity develops for the mutual struggle toward justice, liberation and reconciliation.
- There are also cases in which both the powerful and the weak consider each other guilty. In these cases forgiveness requires mutual repentance accompanied by solidarity and the struggle toward justice and liberation.
- In each case of forgiveness, mutual reconciliation is the goal. In cases where forgiveness is offered but repentance is not evident, reconciliation remains incomplete. In the case of a lack of repentance, the innocent party can keep the door open and in this sense live with a clean conscience—and also begin the journey to personal healing. But the innocent one still suffers from the fruit of the other's non-repentance. In these cases the beneficiaries of forgiveness are not the others but the innocent ones themselves, who are able to break free from the chain that binds them, leave behind the sense of responsibility toward the oppressor and experience a degree of liberation.

It is also important to identify some common myths regarding Christian forgiveness.

Myth #1: To forgive is to forget
This is not true. The impact and power of sin committed against someone is often too strong to forget. The abuse of a child, the trauma suffered by the wife of a murder victim, the destruction of a marriage, the torture allowed by dictators, the injustice of imposed

regimes, the death of a child killed as a result of a drunkard's neglect—these sins are not forgotten. They are events that affect survi-
vors' lives forever. One cannot replace home, family and tranquillity.
The dead do not rise. These sins bring radical changes, and to try to
enter a process of forgiveness in cases like this does not mean to
forget. The power of sin is too strong to be forgotten.

How many times have I heard someone desperately cry, "His
face always comes to my mind. Does this mean I still have not forgiven?" No, that is not what it means! It is normal to remember.
How could we not recall the trauma of loss? Jesus asks us to remember his torture, unjust treatment, passion and death. In the Greek,
Jesus' request literally means not to forget, that is, to remember. But
the same Greek word means truth. To remember is to find the truth.
The truth is found by remembering the past. The Lord's Supper
helps us to remember and to find the truth of God. To remember
does not imply a lack of forgiveness.

Myth #2: Forgiveness is possible only after restitution
This is not true. The cost of sin is not payable. How could one pay
the cost of a life, of a rape or of a divorce? One can make some
measure of payment; one can offer a symbol of repentance; one
can commit to a change of life; one can make promises not to repeat what has been done. These commitments should form part of
the process. But after all is said and done, the cost of sin cannot be
repaid. One characteristic of sin is precisely that it is so serious that
the consequences cannot be undone. Neither does forgiveness undo
the sin committed. But forgiveness does propose an alternative so
that the sin itself does not become an ulcer and does not further
infect lives. Forgiveness delineates a way out for a debt that cannot
be paid.

Myth #3: To forgive means justice has been achieved
I do not believe so. In some cases justice is not possible. Perhaps
guilty parties have already died. Maybe they simply persist in their
sinful ways. Perhaps they reject efforts to compensate for the committed sin. Forgiveness does not guarantee justice; forgiveness does
guarantee that not everyone will remain forever chained to the sin of
the past.

Myth #4: To forgive is easy

It is not. To forgive is to absorb the guilt of another in order to liberate the other. This is one of the most difficult things there is. To forgive is to heal oneself in such a way that the other's guilt does not continue to make one a victim forever. Forgiveness is not easy, especially if there is no indication of repentance in the other's life. Sometimes to forgive is to place the issue of justice for the guilty into God's hands. Even this is never easy because one can always argue that if God did not deliver justice to the victim in the past, there is no guarantee that God will do so now or in the future.

Myth #5: To forgive is to reconcile oneself with the other

Not always. Reconciliation and forgiveness are not synonymous. Reconciliation of two (or more) parties should be always the goal, the last stage, the hope, and in all cases a step that is sought. But it is not always attainable. Perhaps the guilty oppressor has already died, perhaps it is not one person who is guilty but a whole system or structure, perhaps the structure or system or person has not changed or repented, or perhaps the results of sins committed continue to do harm in the present. Despite the goal of reconciliation, in these cases reconciliation cannot be realized. Does this mean victims must surrender before these injustices? Never. Victims continue to struggle for the repentance and transformation of the guilty party in order to improve the future. Does lack of reconciliation mean the victim cannot forgive in these cases? I do not believe so. I have seen many people enter the struggle for justice, and do so with peace and joy, without hatred or rancor, with serenity and confidence in their rights; such people exemplify having forgiven without having achieved the desired reconciliation. A good example can be seen in the attitudes in Latin America toward the Spanish conquistadors of the sixteenth century. Sins committed in that time continue to affect the fortunes of Latin America's inhabitants today. And, with few exceptions, the repercussions are negative. Some remain paralyzed, while others struggle for change with hatred and vengeance. Others work with a certain tranquility but strong commitment to counteract the results of the conquest.

Perhaps the message of the Gospel of John can clarify what we are saying. This gospel shows a double reality that we all experience.

On one hand, it shows God's love for the world—"For God so loved the world" (John 3:16). On the other, this is the world that opposes God the most. How can God continue in this love for the world when the world itself rejects God? The answer lies in the issue of forgiveness. God has forgiven the world before the world recognized, asked for or responded to God's love. God is not a slave to the world's evil. God has already forgiven and waits and works for the repentance of the world, so that justice becomes a reality.

The apostle Paul has something similar in mind when he says:

> But God proves his love for us in that while we still were sinners Christ died for us. . . . For if while we were enemies, we were reconciled to God through the death of his Son, much more surely, having been reconciled, will we be saved by his life. (Rom. 5:8, 10)

Although Paul does not use the word *forgiveness* in this passage, the idea sounds familiar. God loves us; God loves the world so much, even when we are sinners, that God gives his Son for humanity. The powerful and innocent God extends mercy and grace to weak and guilty humanity. God has forgiven. God can love us while we are in sin. God awaits our repentance and transformation so that there may be complete justice and reconciliation.

Myth #6: Forgiveness is automatic and obligatory
Jesus' great commandment for the church speaks of binding and loosing the sins of the world. What do these concepts mean? To loosen is probably easiest to understand. To loosen and to forgive are synonymous. To loosen is to liberate the other from a committed sin, and in doing so to say that both parties are ready to start over again. To bind has a different connotation. It means saying to sin that we are not liberating it yet. That is, other requirements need to be fulfilled before the sin or the sinner can be loosed. Although the text does not say so, I believe these requirements have to do with repentance, transformation and the sound commitment to not repeat walking in the same direction. Forgiveness has demands, requirements, and it expects something from the other party.

Let's return for a moment to the cases suggested at the beginning of this chapter to see whether this analysis helps us.

Dictatorship

It is clear that the oppression caused by military regimes in Latin America is a classic case of the powerful and guilty over and against the innocent and weak. What are the requirements for forgiveness in these cases? True, the case is complicated, because it deals with individuals as well as structures and systems. According to our picture the powerful and guilty have a double task: to repent and to struggle for justice. The innocent also have a double task: to demand repentance and to manage their own bitterness so that they can offer mercy and grace in such a way that the spiral of injustices does not continue.

What does repentance mean in these cases? Individuals in the military need to renounce the military structure, show transformation and give themselves to the struggle for justice. To demonstrate repentance, the military structure needs to redefine its goals, strategies and role. A repentant military has to leave behind arbitrary decision-making, corruption, violent values and hierarchical process. In other words, the guilty party needs to change everything that made it oppressive in the first place. How great it would be if both parties would do their part and so struggle for justice, liberation and the reconciliation of everyone.

Physical/sexual abuse

Physical/sexual abuse is another case of the powerful and guilty against the innocent and weak. Repentance involves the same steps mentioned in the previous case. The goal, reconciliation, is only achieved if all steps are faithfully demonstrated. For the guilty party to ask for forgiveness, the petition must be accompanied by evidence of repentance. Has the person done what is necessary to ensure that these evil acts will not be repeated? The innocent person's struggle is to find personal healing. In the process both parties may find that their struggle for justice has intensified and their ability to offer mercy and grace has also grown.

Capital punishment

In this case we have the guilty and powerful (the murderer), the innocent and weak (the survivor of the victim), and the innocent and powerful (the State). Although our approach could be applied at an individual-individual level, the level of the State proves difficult.

Generally the State does not function from a perspective of forgiveness but from the standpoint of punitive justice. It either punishes or liberates, but it does not consider the liberation of the one who, according to its law, is guilty and deserves punishment. The repentance of the guilty party does not affect the State's process. As a result, we really cannot consider capital punishment an example of Christian spirituality. The basis of capital punishment lies outside the Christian process. The State tends to define justice as the process of just rewards. Christian forgiveness is excluded from this definition because biblical forgiveness always considers the possibility of offering something we do not deserve. Christian forgiveness points toward the repentance and reconciliation of the guilty. The State points toward the deserved punishment of the guilty and the deserved liberation of the innocent. Punitive justice does not consider the liberation of the guilty. This system of punishment and the Christian values of forgiveness, then, are antagonistic systems.

The spirituality of forgiveness proposes an alternative to the world. It is a spirit that is difficult to hear. Nonetheless, Christian mission continues to minister within the sinful world, pointing toward its reconciliation with God (see 2 Cor. 5:11–21). We still struggle with the temptation of Jonah: to preach the judgment and punishment of God and to rebel against the mercy and grace God wants to reveal to those who repent. Sometimes, like Jonah, we prefer the shade of the tree to the grace and compassion of God.

Part 6

25

The spirit of the poor, the poor in the Spirit

❦

Blessed are the poor in spirit. (Matt. 5:3a)

Throughout history many powerful and wealthy people have manipulated, mistreated and taken advantage of this saying of Jesus. The poor are blessed? Great! Let's keep them poor so they can truly enjoy this blessing of poverty! By becoming rich we are participating in God's will, pouring blessings upon the poor! Everyone wins!

Some Bible translations attempt to improve this image of the poor slightly by spiritualizing the translation:

Happy are those who know they are spiritually poor;
the Kingdom of heaven belongs to them! (Matt. 5:3,
Good News Bible)

This translation contains many problems:
- the Greek text does not include the verb meaning "to know";
- the word "poor," when translated as the phrase "those who know they are spiritually poor," reduces poor to poor spiritually. The parallel text in Luke does not allow this kind of spiritualization of the teaching, and I doubt it fits here in Matthew (see Luke 6:20); and

- the Greek text does not use the word for "spirit" as an adjective but as a noun.

The New Revised Standard Version translators chose to omit the article "the" that occurs in the Greek in front of "spirit." This omission changes the meaning of the phrase in English. Instead of saying "Blessed are the poor in the spirit (the poor who walk in the spirit)," it says "Blessed are the poor in spirit (those who have a poor spirit)."

Although the translators explain that the article often disappears while using the dative case, it seems that, in this case, the impact in English is too strong to justify the omission. It would make more sense to affirm that there is a spirit within poverty upon which the new kingdom is also founded. Jesus seems to have said that the poor have a spiritual blessing, that something in the context of the poor allows them to open themselves to God, and that they reflect a spirituality closer to that of God than the spirituality of the rich. At least this is consistent with other words spoken by Jesus. Some have suggested this phrase might mean the "spirit of the poor"; that is, that the poor recognize their dependence on others, understand human interdependence, see the evil of oppression, comprehend that their situation is unjust and struggle for the change they deserve. In other words, the spirit of the poor is a blessed spirituality.

The Greek might also be translated, "Blessed are the poor *through* the spirit." This translation states that it is the presence of the Spirit that places the poor in a blessed position; when the Spirit of God enters, the poor are the fortunate ones, the blessed. This idea concurs with the announcement of Jesus:

> "The Spirit of the Lord is upon me,
> because he has anointed me to bring good news to
> the poor." (Luke 4:18a)

A third possible translation also corresponds with the idea suggested here: "Blessed are the poor *with* the spirit."

This translation is similar to the other two. The poor with the spirit, the poor in the spirit, and the poor through the spirit—these three possibilities express more completely the meaning of Jesus' phrase.

Jesus' first word also deserves careful attention. The translation "blessed" uses a passive tense. The poor, sitting on the margins
in their poverty, passively receive or have the blessing of God. But it
is also possible to understand this word from another perspective.

Elias Chacour, a Palestinian author well-versed in Semitic languages (see Chacour, 143–44), suggests that a word in Aramaic,
Jesus' mother tongue, lies behind the Greek phrasing. He proposes
that Jesus, probably speaking in Aramaic, used the word *ashray*,
from the verb *yashar*. *Yashar* and *ashray* are very active words,
meaning to act, move, turn around, repent or put oneself on the
road. Combining this suggestion with the previous ones, this phrase
could be translated:

> May the poor get up, move, walk and act in-with-
> through the spirit, for theirs is the kingdom of heaven.

Understood from this perspective, this phrase rings true with other
teachings of Jesus.
- It affirms that the Spirit is with the poor.
- It suggests that the Spirit of the poor fits very well within the
  coming kingdom of God.
- It encourages the poor to move in the direction of the kingdom
  that has arrived.
- It suggests that as the poor move toward the kingdom, the
  kingdom will also be revealed in the world.

The parallel text in Luke has a different focus. It says:

> "Blessed are you who are poor,
>> for yours is the kingdom of God." (Luke 6:20)

I will highlight two differences in Luke and Matthew:
1. Luke's text does not refer to "in spirit."
2. Luke's text speaks to the disciples in the second person
   (you, yours) and not in the third person (they, theirs), as in
   the passage from Matthew.

Let's begin with the second observation, because it explains
the first. In this text Jesus speaks directly to the disciples (6:17, 20),
who are poor. How does Jesus know his disciples are poor? Because renouncing wealth had been part of their calling. When Jesus
said, "Follow me," the disciples responded immediately:

> When they had brought their boats to shore, they left
> everything and followed him. (Luke 5:11)

Levi the tax collector also "got up, left everything, and fol-
lowed him" (Luke 5:28).

In Luke, then, the blessing is the blessing of being a disciple.
Not just any kind of disciple, however, but a disciple who had already
left everything to follow Jesus. This phrase in Luke, then, presupposes renouncing wealth as part of the integral commitment of discipleship.

This may clarify Matthew's phrase "in spirit." In his own way
Luke has made clear what poor in spirit means. It means to understand the call to discipleship as a call that has strong implications for
our wallets, our riches and our goods. Those who renounce their
right to wealth can "love [their] enemies" (Luke 6:27), "bless those
who curse [them]" (Luke 6:28), "do good to those who hate [them]"
(Luke 6:27), "pray for those who abuse [them]" (Luke 6:28), "offer
the other [cheek] also" (Luke 6:29, RSV) and "give to everyone who
begs from [them]" (Luke 6:30). The rich cannot enter into this blessing because they have not been willing to respond to a discipleship
that also commits their wallet. The disciple who has responded with
everything is the disciple who fits well into the nature of the kingdom, because the kingdom of God does not stay out of the economic realm.

It may be that the spiritual poverty of which Matthew's text
speaks, the poor in the spirit, and the disciple who has renounced
his or her commitment to wealth, are one and the same. It could be
that the spirit of the poor disciple, the disciple who has understood
following Jesus as renouncing economic security, is, at the same
time, the poor in (with) the spirit.

Luke also emphasizes the words of Jesus in Nazareth, saying
that when "the Spirit of the Lord" had fallen "upon [him]" (Luke
4:18), Jesus declares "good news to the poor" (Luke 4:18). There is
no doubt that the announcement of the kingdom is good news for
the poor. Not because other poor people come to share the poverty, but because the situation of the poor will improve with the
presence of the kingdom.

What should become clear is that the kingdom of God neither
justifies nor desires nor blesses poverty *as such*. Poverty will be one

of the problems treated and rectified with the coming of the king-dom. The world's spirit of wealth will be extinguished by the critique that comes out of poverty.

Thus the spirit of the poor is one of the spirits of the new kingdom that has arrived in Jesus. The poor are both the principal subject of the inauguration of the new kingdom and the necessary object of its benefits. Only when the spirit of the poor feels at home in the world, accommodates itself in many people's lives and be-comes present in the logic of the economic system do the poor in the spirit really become the beneficiaries, the ones blessed by the coming of the kingdom.

What does all of this have to do with Christian spirituality and mission? Liberation theology has highlighted the role of the poor in God's plan. Roman Catholic bishops have said that the poor are in a "preferential" position for God's acting in history. God is on the side of the poor, in their difficult situation, to encourage them in their struggle and to transform their conditions (see the documents from the Second General Conference of Bishops of Latin America and the Third General Conference of Bishops of Latin America, held at Medellín in 1968 and Puebla in 1979, respectively, listed in the bibliography). God opposes the oppressors, the wealthy and the powerful, who struggle to keep the situation as it is.

According to Jesus' teaching, the poor are in a favored posi-tion. This is so for two reasons. First, the coming of the kingdom of God in Jesus is to change the situation of the poor radically. Their situation will be transformed because the lack of equality, the op-pression and the hunger and mistreatment that we understand as part of the situation of the poor in our world do not coincide with the character of this kingdom. Truly, the poor will be blessed with the coming of the kingdom. The power of God is on the side of the poor.

Second, one who is poor is, at the same time, the principal subject of this change. The spirituality found in poverty is closely aligned with the spirituality God requires to enter the kingdom. To recognize the injustice that surrounds us, to discern the roots of oppression, to depend on the direction of the Holy Spirit, to share what little one has with the needy, to open oneself to new revela-tions of God and to recognize one's dependence on God and our human interdependence are only some of the characteristics already present in the world of the poor and in the purpose of the kingdom of God. As protagonist and object, then, the poor are the ones who are blessed with the coming of God's kingdom.

Our spirituality must be aligned with that of the poor for it to be Christian. This teaching of Jesus cuts to the heart of the evils of the modern world and also points to their defeat. The kingdom of God is a transforming power. Christian spirituality must align itself with this transformation or lose its relevance for the world.

Christian mission is the mission of transformation. Sometimes it will be changed hearts that transform structures, but we cannot deny that transformed structures also change the hearts of people who live in and under them. Christian mission has many fronts: evangelizing people, structures and systems. The affirmations that the "Spirit of the Lord is upon me," and also that the poor are "blessed" in the Spirit do not leave us any neutral ground. Our spirituality and our mission must be oriented to these affirmations in order for them to be Christian.❦

26

The Spirit groans, creation groans: Do we groan?

Does groaning have anything to do with Christian spirituality and mission?

One of the most beautiful chapters in the New Testament, focused on the victorious life in the Spirit, centers on groaning.

The relationship between the victorious spiritual life and the process of groaning is illustrated in Romans 8.

Characteristics of the victorious life in the Spirit (Rom. 8:2–24)
- the Spirit is a "Spirit of life"
- the intention of the Spirit is "life and peace"
- "the Spirit is life because of righteousness"
- the Spirit of the resurrection will "give life" to us
- the Spirit makes us "joint heirs with Christ"
- the Spirit gives hope
- the Spirit opposes sin, death, the flesh, slavery, fear and decay

The trio of those who groan

Creation groans (8:22): Paul argues that we who have the Spirit of life, peace and justice, are the new sons and daughters of God, heirs of God and joint heirs with Christ (8:16–17). He immediately continues:

> For the creation waits with eager longing for the re-
> vealing of the children of God: for the creation was
> subjected to futility. (8:19–20a)

> We know that the whole creation has been groaning
> in labor pains until now. (8:22)

How incredible! Creation burns with the hope that we will act in its
favor! Creation has suffered continuous birth pains waiting for us to
reveal ourselves as related to God! Creation begs to be

> set free from its bondage to decay and will obtain the
> freedom of the glory of the children of God. (8:21)

Our spirituality has to do with the liberation of creation. Our mission
liberates creation from its enslavement, from its bondage to decay.

We groan (8:23): We, born of the Spirit as sons and daughters
of hope (8:14–17, 24–25), also wait for the "redemption of our
bodies" (8:23). We groan as one with creation (8:23). There is a
direct relationship between the redemption of our bodies and the
liberation of creation from its bondage. Our redemption simultaneously liberates creation! And the liberation of creation redeems
us! The two redemptions and the two liberations go hand in hand,
like flesh and blood. We know our weaknesses, but at the same time
we understand our hope (8:25–26). Our weak activity gains power
and importance within the hope toward which the Spirit guides us
(8:26).

And the Spirit groans (8:26):

> Likewise the Spirit helps us in our weakness; for we
> do not know how to pray as we ought, but that very
> Spirit intercedes with sighs too deep for words. And
> God, who searches the heart, knows what is the mind
> of the Spirit, because the Spirit intercedes for the saints
> according to the will of God. (8:26–27)

Creation groans with pain, we groan in weakness and the Holy
Spirit groans within us, guiding us in discernment. What about God?

What does God do? According to this passage, God searches our hearts and finds the groaning's purpose. God listens to the groaning of the Spirit in our favor. In this process God shows us God's power, trust and love; and nothing,

> neither death, nor life, nor angels, nor rulers, nor things present, nor things to come, nor powers, nor height, nor depth, nor anything else in all creation, will be able to separate us from the love of God in Christ Jesus our Lord. (8:38)

These comforting words provide a hopeful promise. But beyond the beauty of this divine solidarity with us is our mission: to help with the birth, to push and pull so the new baby may be born. Creation's groaning and our own groaning is not a gimmick, nor is it to complain of our bad luck or to lament a difficult situation. This groaning means to implore, beg and intercede in favor of creation. This supplication is active, an intervention, a mission. Again we see that our spirituality is personal and social, our holiness is personal and creational, our mission is personal and structural and our commitment is personal and systemic.

Once again we see Christian mission as inseparable from its spirituality. We are midwives of new realities. Just as the birth of a child is inevitable after nine months, so too the birth of a new creation is the sure fruit of our birthing mission, a mission based in the Spirit of Jesus Christ.

27

The spirit of hope, the hope of the Spirit

Christian spirituality and mission are held together by Christian hope. A popular saying is, The last thing you lose is hope.

The apostle Peter says:

> Always be ready to make your defense to anyone who demands from you an accounting for the hope that is in you. (1 Pet. 3:15b)

Paul says:

> For in [with, for] hope we were saved. Now hope that is seen is not hope. (Rom. 8:24)

The author of Hebrews says:

> Let us hold fast to the confession of our hope without wavering. (Heb. 10:23a)

> Now faith is the assurance of things hoped for, the conviction of things not seen, (Heb. 11:1)

Colossians says:

Christ in you, the hope of glory. (Col. 1:27)

Paul says:

"I am on trial concerning the hope of the resurrection
of the dead." (Acts 23:6)

Speaking about the power of God, Paul says that it is God

who gives life to the dead and calls into existence the
things that do not exist. (Rom. 4:17)

Hope is basic—we read of Abraham that "hoping against hope,
he believed (Rom. 4:18)—but the concept of hope as such has received bad press in the last few centuries. Why? Let's look at some
critiques leveled against Christian hope.[1]

Perhaps the most famous criticism is that by Karl Marx—"Re-
ligion is the opiate of the people." How can this be? Concentrating
on the future, in the hope of another world, takes away the energy
of the faithful to transform the present world. Nourishing ourselves
with concerns for the future, Christian hope diverts our attention
from the present, twists our transforming strength, and distances us
from true Christian activity. That is, Christian hope is responsible
for Christian indifference, laziness and inefficiency.

Pascal, a French philosopher and scientist, has said that Christian hope makes it so that we never live but we always hope to live;
we always prepare to live, but we never concentrate on life in the
present.

Goethe, the German poet, suggests that the present contains
its own eternity. The human being is only able to experience the
present; the past and the future cannot really be known. Searching
for eternity in the present moment is what gives flavor and importance to life. Christian hope tends to become an obstacle for our
attention to the present time.

---

[1] The following is a summary of some important observations made
by Jürgen Moltmann in *Theology of Hope*. See the introduction to that
work for a more detailed analysis.

Nietzsche, the German philosopher, claimed that to find love of the eternal is loyalty to the earth.

Søren Kierkegaard spoke of the Christian as the believer who makes himself completely present in the present. Believing, the Christian gets tomorrow off his back. The future is in the hands of God; we just stay with the worries of the present.

And sometimes we hear it said that Christians are so heavenly minded that they are no earthly good or that with their souls in heaven, Christians forget that their feet are on the ground.

There are many critiques of Christian hope, and we must admit at the outset that if our hope does not energize us to live the present more profoundly and more significantly, then it is not true Christian hope.

But the richness of Christian hope can keep us from falling into the faults the critics identify. Let's look at some important observations from Moltmann:

- looking at the future, Christian hope moves toward this future, and in this movement transforms the present;
- Christian hope is not the end of Christianity but its beginning; it is not the sunset but the sunrise;
- Christian hope emerges from the present reality and announces this reality's future under the power of God;
- upon announcing the future reality, Christian hope provides a promise for the present;
- to act according to this promise in the present transforms the present reality;
- Christian hope is the active expectation of things that, by faith, we see as God's promises;
- from history, Christian hope knows that the Resurrection was the future of the Crucified One, and by faith understands that this same future awaits redeemed humanity;
- by living according to God's promise, Christian hope will oppose the reality of the present;
- those who hope in Christ begin to challenge the present reality;
- this is how peace with God means conflict with the world;
- this is how the promise and the hope of God destabilize the unjust reality of the present;
- if God "calls into existence the things that do not exist" (Rom. 4:17), and if the community of God continues to follow this calling, then the present changes;

- to love the enemy treats someone as a companion who is not yet one; that is, it challenges us to love "things that do not exist as if they did";
- this love of the nonexistent is the divine power that transforms the reality of the nonexistent and proclaims the presence of a new possibility for the world.

Moltmann identifies two principal enemies of Christian hope. The first enemy is pretension or assumption. To assume is to anticipate prematurely that which we hope of God. What we anticipate prematurely is not fulfilled because we do not participate and do our part. Pretension is premature triumphalism. Waiting for the triumph of God, we do not commit ourselves to the path of God's promises. In this way, hope *does* become the opiate of the people.

The second enemy of hope is despair. Despair is arbitrarily and prematurely to surrender what we hoped for from God. To despair is to announce that what we have been hoping for will not be accomplished.

Both enemies of hope take us to the same destination. Both are grounded in realism as the only trustworthy source to ground our action. Pretension accommodates itself to reality because it believes God's promise will soon be fulfilled; despair resigns itself to reality because it no longer hopes for anything new. Both end up being champions of "realism." Thus, both enemies guide us toward inaction, silence and indifference. In each case the sins of omission, rather than those of action, cry out before God.

Let's look at some examples to make this clearer. God promises us a new creation, but we do not consider ourselves capable of living according to its characteristics; we surrender prematurely before God's promise. God honors us with promises of justice and peace, and we celebrate their coming arbitrarily and prematurely. God wants us to act with the things that do not exist as if they did. And God asks us to act with other things that do exist as if they did not. Pretension and despair remain grounded in reality, in that which does exist and with that which does not exist. In both cases, the transformation of the present is impossible.

But there is another element of Christian hope. The authors of the New Testament insist that hope is invisible:

Now hope that is seen is not hope. (Rom. 8:24b)

> Now faith is the assurance of things hoped for, the
> conviction of things not seen. (Heb. 11:1)

> [God] gives life to the dead and calls into existence the
> things that do not exist. (Rom. 4:17)

If hope is invisible, how can it be so important? This question
is anticipated as well. The author of Hebrews tells us that the acts of
faith, founded on hope, *are* visible.

Faith is "the assurance of hope." Faith is "the conviction of
hope." The author also calls us to the "confession of our hope without wavering" (Heb. 10:23). The Greek here implies that we search
for ways to "make visible" the hope that we have: to justify it, defend
it, teach it and show it. We could say that these Scriptures call us to
a pedagogy of hope in the world for which the hope remains invisible. Each act of faith, putting into practice the "fruit" of the Spirit,
and each explanation of why we act in this way, is a pedagogy of
Christian hope. This is how something that is invisible becomes visible and understandable for the world. The Christian task is to act
visibly according to the invisible hope that is within us.

Once again Paul's brilliant phrase attracts us. God is a God
who treats things that do not exist as though they already do. This is
another way of saying that, as Christians, we act according to the
invisible hope as if it were already real. Hope is the Christian's new
reality. The invisible things are those which, by faith, we understand
to be sure and trustworthy. They are trustworthy enough so that we
can act according to their premises in the present. It's an unbeliev-
able ministry, isn't it?

Anticipating the world's reaction, the Bible's authors incorporate two more characteristics into the ministry of hope. We need to
have patience and perseverance.

> Keep alert and always persevere . . . for all the saints.
> (Eph. 6:18)

> Keep alert, stand firm in your faith, be courageous, be
> strong. (1 Cor. 16:13)

> He has now reconciled [you]—provided that you con-
> tinue securely established and steadfast in the faith,

without shifting from the hope promised by the gospel that you heard. (Col. 1:22–23a)

But the one who endures to the end will be saved. (Matt. 24:13)

We boast in our hope . . . we also boast in our sufferings, knowing that suffering produces endurance, and endurance produces character, and character produces hope. (Rom. 5:2b–4)

Thus there is a fourfold manifestation of the Spirit: the invisible foundation is *hope*; *faith* reveals hope in visible and defendable actions, that is, it serves as the pedagogy of hope; *patience* and *perseverance* nourish faith, in the knowledge that to act with things that do not exist as if they already did would be seen as "insanity," generating suspicion and creating conflict. Hope, faith, patience and perseverance make up an indivisible team. The absence of one destroys the whole. Without perseverance we are pretentious; without patience we despair; without faith we are idle and indifferent; and without hope we conform to reality. The status quo is happy to see the pretension, despair, indifference and conformity of Christians. This guarantees that reality will remain unchanged. But the kingdom of God calls us to hope, faith, perseverance and patience. This is how the power of God reveals itself and the present is transformed.

The spirituality of Christian hope becomes the mission of Christian hope.

Epilogue

The thesis of this book is simple. Christian spirituality means to align oneself with the Spirit of God; Christian mission is to align oneself with the activity of God. Since it is the Spirit of God that founds God's mission, and it is the mission of God that reveals its Spirit, Christian spirituality and Christian mission are inseparable and indivisible.

Sometimes we mistakenly believe that spirituality is mystical while mission is active. The principal measurement is neither mysticism nor activism. The most sure measurement is Christ, who is accessible to us in the Sacred Scriptures. Does our mysticism guide us to act as Christ acted? Does our activism bring us to think as Christ thought?

We should not think that manifestations of Christian spirituality and Christian mission are always sequential: first prayer and then action; first the clamor and then victory; first doubt and then trust; first tears and then happiness; first despair and then hope. We seldom experience life organized so neatly. Evidence shows that these manifestations are parallel not sequential experiences; they are simultaneous feelings and actions and are not ordered chronologically. Recognizing this reality allows us to move on, even in valleys of shadows, and keeps us in a posture of humility, even in moments of triumph. I want to conclude with a biblical expression in which we see these multiple experiences in the life of the psalmist:

140

How long, O LORD? Will you forget me forever?
   How long will you hide your face from me?
How long must I bear pain in my soul,
   and have sorrow in my heart all day long?
How long shall my enemy be exalted over me?

Consider and answer me, O LORD my God!
   Give light to my eyes, or I will sleep the sleep of
      death,
and my enemy will say, "I have prevailed";
   my foes will rejoice because I am shaken.

But I have trusted in your steadfast love;
   my heart shall rejoice in your salvation.
I will sing to the LORD,
   because he has dealt bountifully with me. (Ps. 13)

    To this complaint, to this clamor, to this search, to this trust and to this celebration, may we daily enjoin our efforts and direct our commitment. Amen.

Bibliography

Bailie, Gil. *Violence Unveiled*. New York: Crossroads, 1995.

Boff, Leonardo. *Faith on the Edge*. San Francisco: Harper & Row, 1989.

———. *Ecclesiogenesis: The Base Communities Reinvent the Church*. Maryknoll, N.Y.: Orbis Books, 1986.

———. *El Padrenuestro*. Madrid: Ediciones Paulinas, 1982.

———. *Iglesia, Carisma y Poder*. Bogotá, 1989.

Boff, Leonardo and Clodovis. *Salvation and Liberation*. Maryknoll, N.Y.: Orbis Books, 1984.

Bonino, J. Míguez. *La Fe en busca de la Eficacia*. Salamanca: Ediciones Sígueme, 1977.

Brueggemann, Walter. *The Prophetic Imagination*. Philadelphia: Fortress Press, 1978.

Castillo, José María. *Teología para Comunidades*. Madrid: Ediciones Paulinas, 1990.

Chacour, Elias. *We Belong to This Land*. San Francisco: Harper, 1990.

Cook, Guillermo. *Profundidad en la Evangelización*. Jenison: Tell, 1989.

De Mello, Anthony. *¿Quién Puede Hacer que Amanezca?*. Santander: Sal Terrae, 1985.

Driver, Juan. *Community and Commitment*. Scottdale: Herald Press, 1976.

———. *El Espíritu Santo en la Comunidad Mesiánica*. Bogotá: Ediciones CLARA-SEMILLA, 1992.

Esperanza en Camino: Del Espiritualismo a la Espiritualidad, no. 7 (March 1989). Guatemala City: Ediciones SEMILLA.

Galilea, Segundo. *El Camino de la Espiritualidad*. Madrid: Ediciones Paulinas, 1984.

———. *El Discipulado Cristiano*. Madrid: Ediciones Paulinas, 1993.

Gammie, John G. *Holiness in Israel*. Minneapolis: Fortress Press, 1989.

Grellert, Manfred. *Los Compromisos de la Misión*. San José: Varitec, 1991.

Grellert, Manfred, Bryant L. Myers, and Thomas H. McAlpine, eds. *Al Servicio del Reino*. San José: Varitec, 1992.

Books with Spanish titles are not available in English.

Grellert, Manfred, and Mariano Avila. *Conversión y Discipulado*. San José: Varitec, 1993.

Griffin, David Ray, ed. *Spirituality and Society*. New York: State University of New York Press, 1988.

Huebner, Harry, and David Schroeder. *Church as Parable: Whatever Happened to Ethics?*. Winnipeg: CMBC Publications, 1993.

Lederach, Juan Pablo. *Seguir a Jesús*. México: Editorial Kyrios, 1993.

Mesters, Carlos. *Esperanza de un Pueblo que Lucha*. Bogotá: Ediciones Paulinas, 1987.

Moltmann, Jürgen. *Theology of Hope*. London: SCM Press, 1967.

Rudolph, Otto. *Das Heilige*, 1917.

Pannenberg, Wolfhart. *La Fe de los Apóstoles*. Salamanca: Ediciones Sígueme, 1974.

Second General Conference of Latin American Bishops, convened at Medellín, Colombia (August 24-September 6, 1968), Final Documents, *The Church in the Present-Day Transformation of Latin America in Light of the Council*, vol. 2, *Conclusions* (Washington, D.C.: U.S. Catholic Conference, 1970).

Steuernagel, Valdir R. *La Misión de la Iglesia*. San José: Varitec, 1992.

Suderman, Roberto J. *El Discipulado Cristiano al Servicio del Reino*. Bogotá: Ediciones CLARA-SEMILLA, 1994.

Third General Conference of Latin American Bishops, convened at Puebla, Mexico, January 1979, *Final Documents*, in *Puebla and Beyond*, ed. John Eagleson and Philip Scharper (Maryknoll, N.Y.: Orbis Books, 1979).

Yoder, John H. *The Politics of Jesus*. Grand Rapids, Mich.: Eerdmans, 1988.

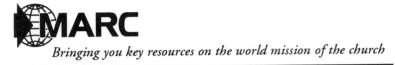

MARC

Bringing you key resources on the world mission of the church

MARC books and other publications support the work of MARC (Mission Advanced Research and Communications Center), which is to inspire vision and empower Christian mission among those who extend the whole gospel to the whole world.

Recent MARC titles include:

▶ *Serving With the Urban Poor: Cases in Holistic Ministry*, Tetsunao Yamamori, Bryant L. Myers and Kenneth L. Luscombe, editors. Case studies from around the world focus on the plight of the urban poor and show how they can come to know the hope of Christ and progress beyond their physical needs.   248 pp. $16.95

▶ *Sexually Exploited Children: Working to Protect and Heal*, Phyllis Kilbourn and Marjorie McDermid, editors. A hands-on, practical resource for people who are ready to respond to the needs of children exploited by the sex industry.   352 pp. $24.95

▶ *Together Again: Kinship of Word and Deed* by Roger S. Greenway. This brief but powerful presentation by one of America's most respected missionary statesmen reunites evangelism and social action under the banner of evangelical missions.   40 pp. $5.95

▶ *Choosing a Future for U.S. Missions* by Paul McKaughan, Dellanna O'Brien and William O'Brien. Takes a hard look at current mission realities and offers promising possibilities for the future of U.S. mission organizations.   128 pp. $11.95

Contact us toll free in the U.S.: 1-800-777-7752
Direct: (626) 301-7720

World Vision

MARC 800 W. Chestnut Ave.
Monrovia, CA
91016-3198 USA

MARC books are published
by World Vision

Ask for the MARC Newsletter and complete publications list